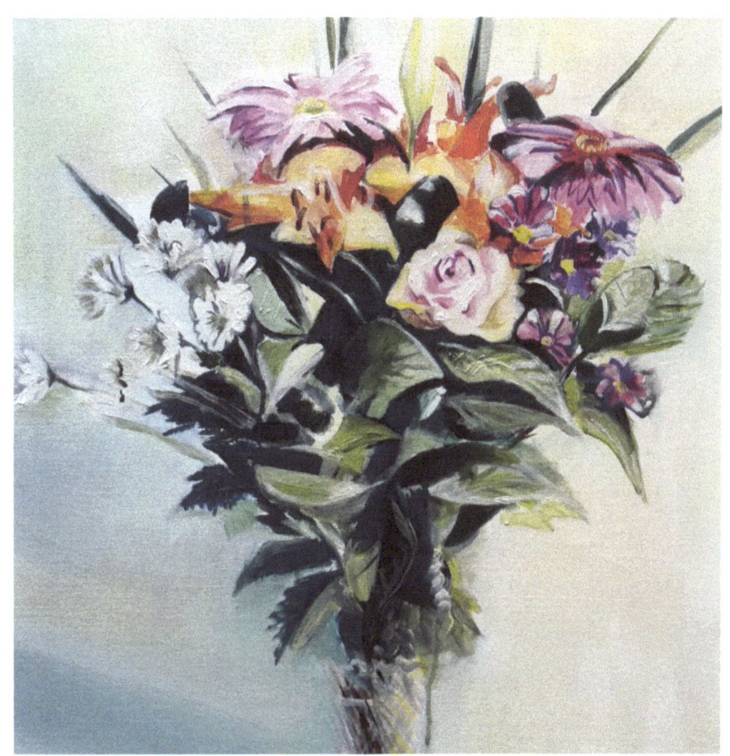

A COLLECTION OF

Paintings & Poetry

OF AUSTRALIAN LANDSCAPE, SEASCAPE & FLORA

Original paintings by Virginia Bucknell

Poetry by Cassa Bassa (Jia-Li Yang)

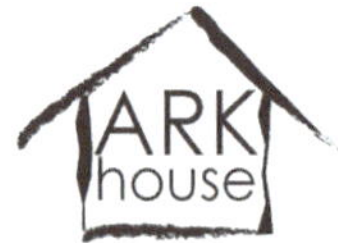

Ark House Press
arkhousepress.com

Cataloguing in Publication Data:
Title: A Collection of Paintings and Poetry of Australian Landscape, Seascape and Flora
ISBN: 978-0-6455947-9-9 (pbk)
Subjects: Poetry; Inspirational;
Other Authors/Contributors: Yang, Jia Li; Bucknell, Virginia

Design by initiateagency.com

Collaboration Story

Virginia and Jia-Li started a friendship and partnership from the inspiration of the beautiful nature created by Mother Earth.

Their love for the Australian landscape, seascape and native flora fuelled their creativity in painting and poetry writing.

This collaboration of paintings and poetry gave them direction, joy and excitement.

May this book give you pleasure and enjoyment.

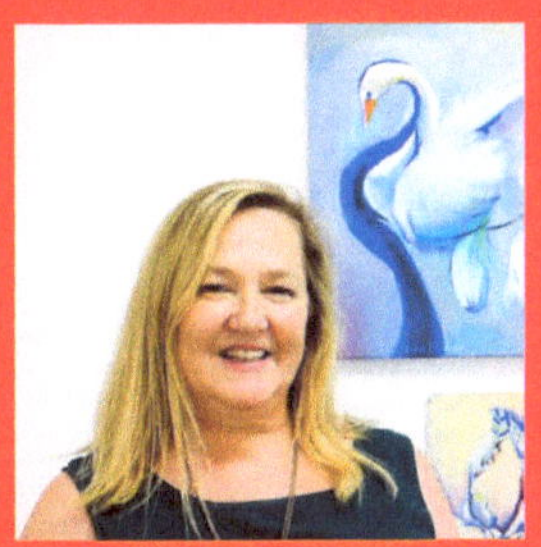

About Virginia

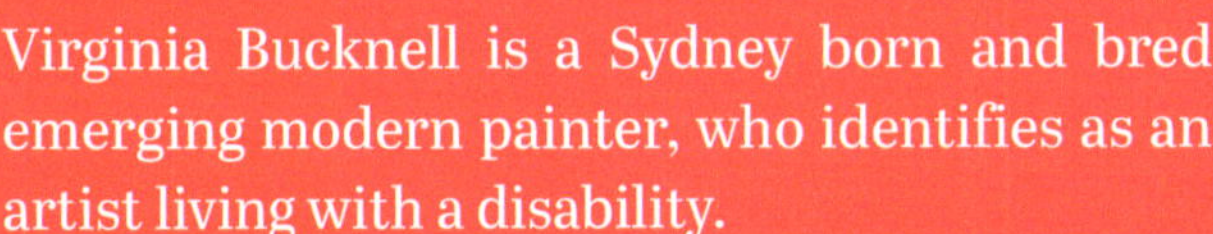

Virginia Bucknell is a Sydney born and bred emerging modern painter, who identifies as an artist living with a disability.

Transitioned from a performance artist to a visual artist, Virginia paints landscape, portrait art and still life inspired by nature's everyday beauty.

Her work is influenced by the French impressionists and abstract artists.

Virginia is a keen observer and precise interpreter of emotions through portraiture.

Through painting, Virginia processes and expresses her unique and at times complex emotions.

The completion of a painting often grants her a sense of clarity.

For more of Virginia's artwork, visit
www.virginiabucknellartwork.weebly.com
Instagram handle **@ginnybee1**

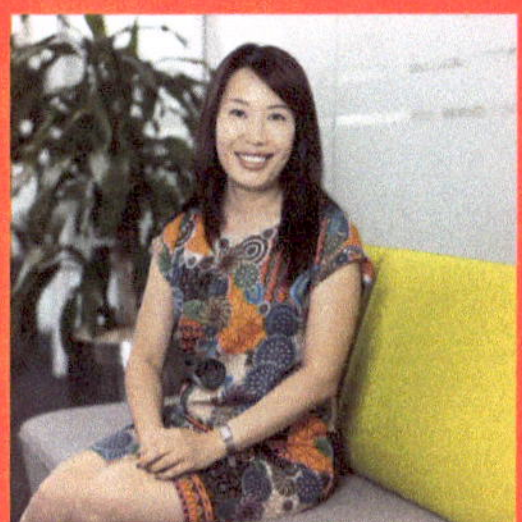

About Jia-li

China born Australian Poet Jia-Li Yang works with the disadvantaged people in the community which gives her a special insight into those that suffer. She is constantly inspired by their resilience and strength.

Jia-Li's poetry has been published in the Australian Poetry Journal; *The Poets Symphony, Creation and the Cosmos* published by Raw Earth Ink; *Heart Beats, Social Justice Inks* published by Prolific Pulse Press; *Wounds I Healed* published by EIF.

Jia-Li blogs under the name Cassa Bassa:
www.flickerofthoughts.com

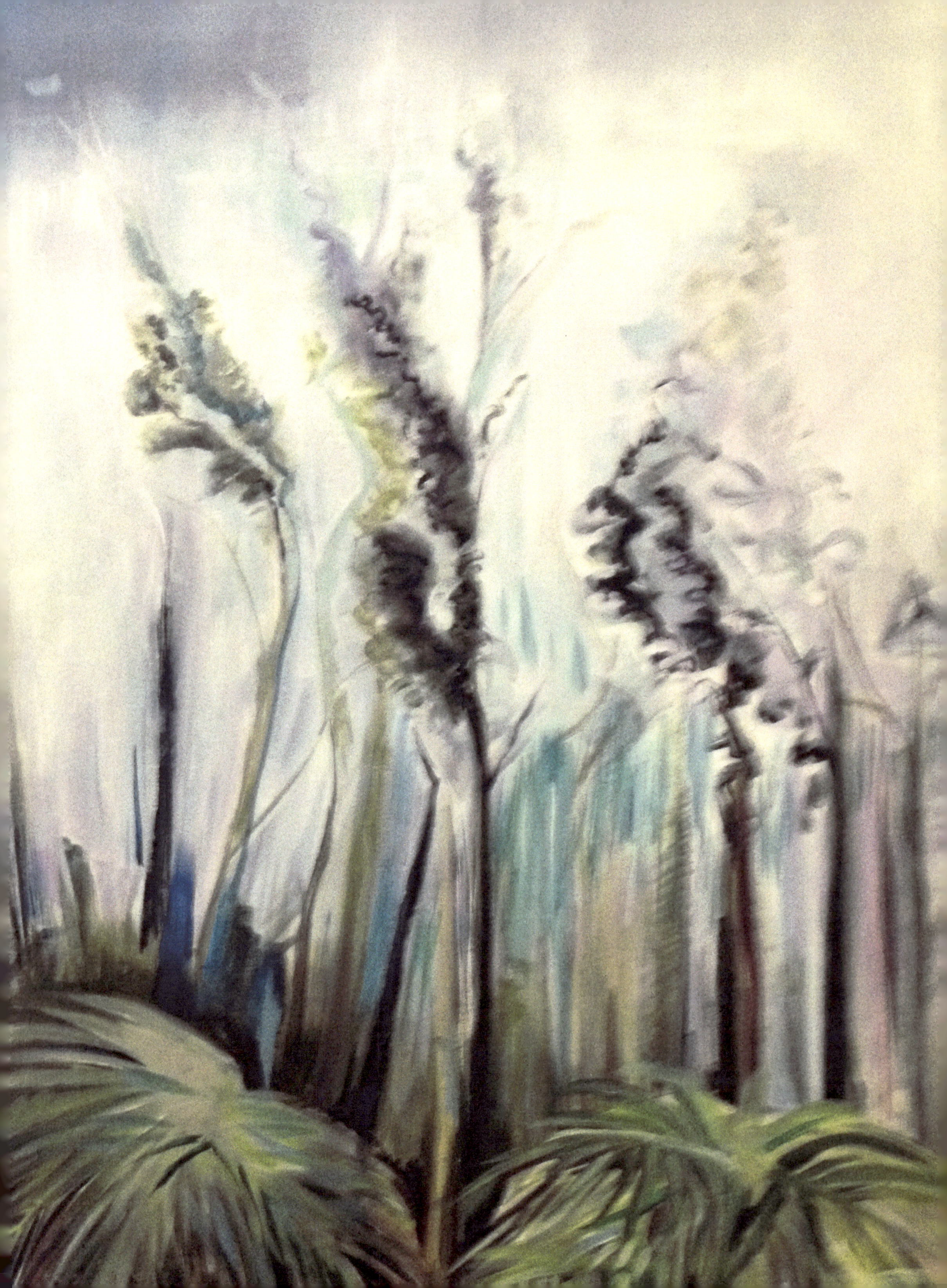

Flora Illusion

Ballerinas in their lilac, indigo
and sage tutus
Dancing in formation of Grand Jeté, Plié, Fouetté
Their striking performance set me off to euphoria

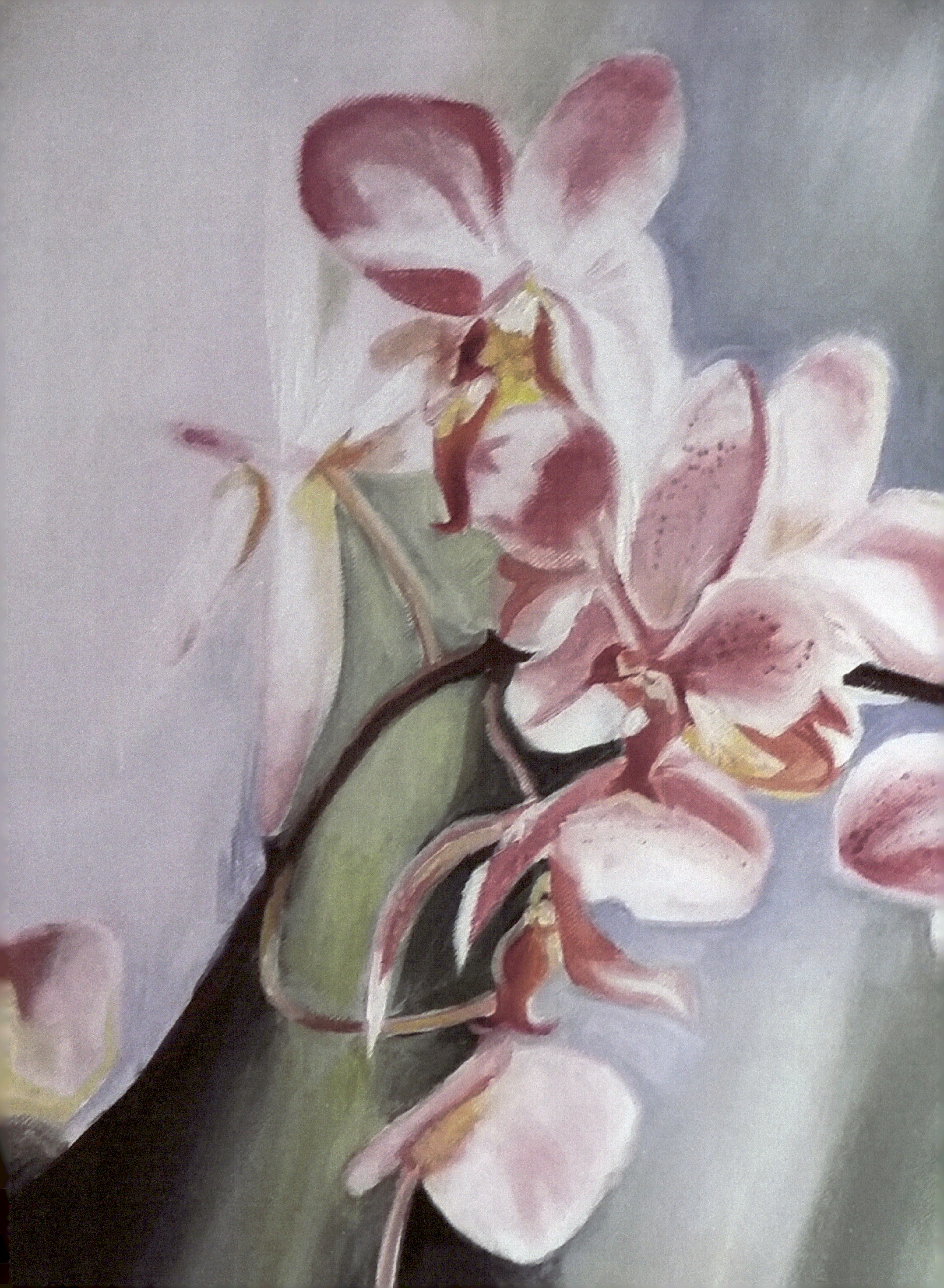

Orchid Bloom

The gentle morning glow
teases you
to let down
your bronze armour

The flush of [illegible]
peeling open [illegible]
enough to make the sun envy

You make peace
by weaving
a piece of yourself
into the light

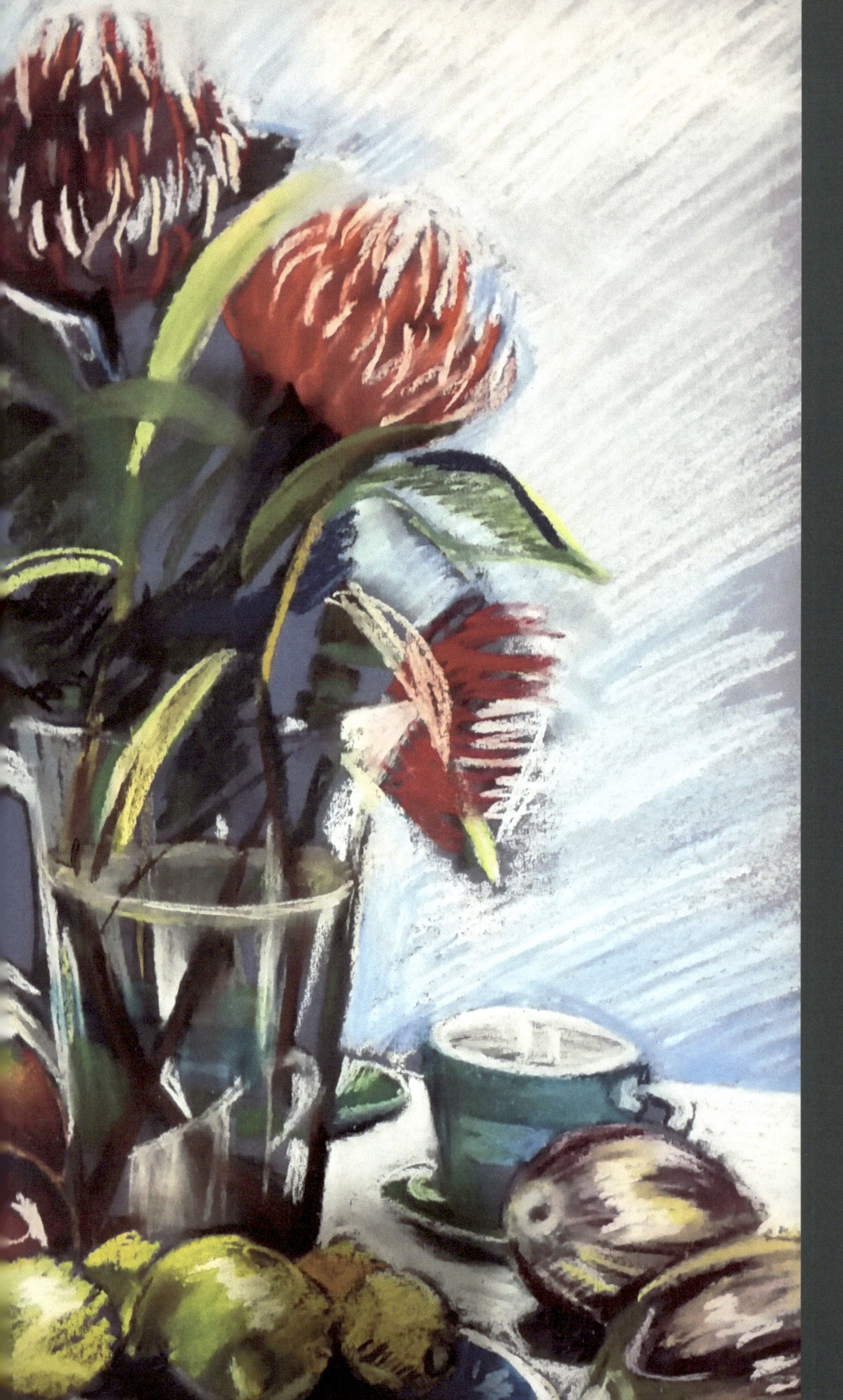

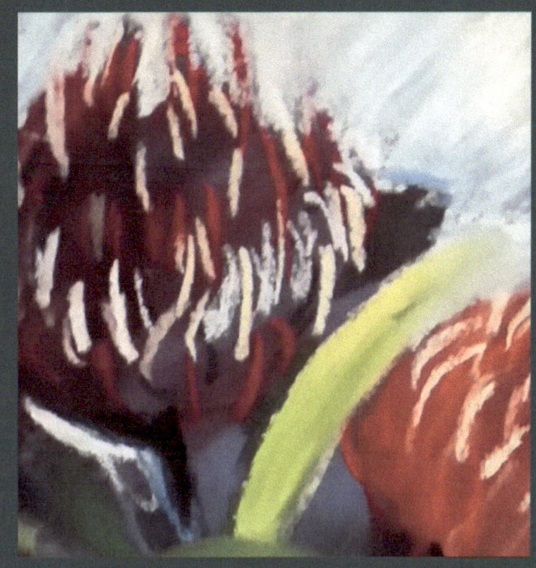

Waratah

You were once white and wild
Crimson bled on your pure form
Guarded by razored leaves
and long sword stem
today you are a domestic icon
well known in every household

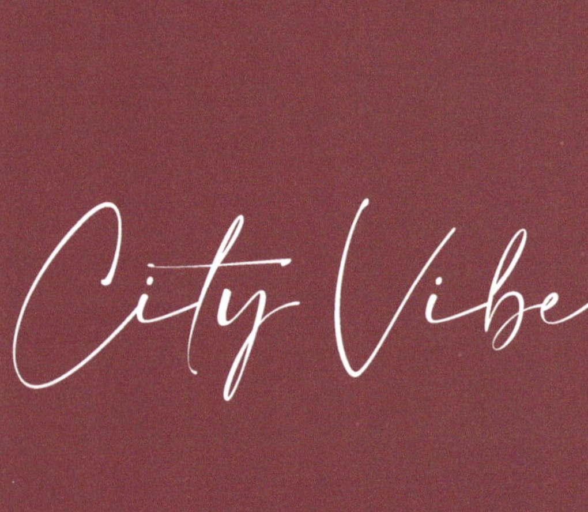

The city never sleeps
Last night's vibrancy
lingers around the morning twilight
flowing into a new day's excitement

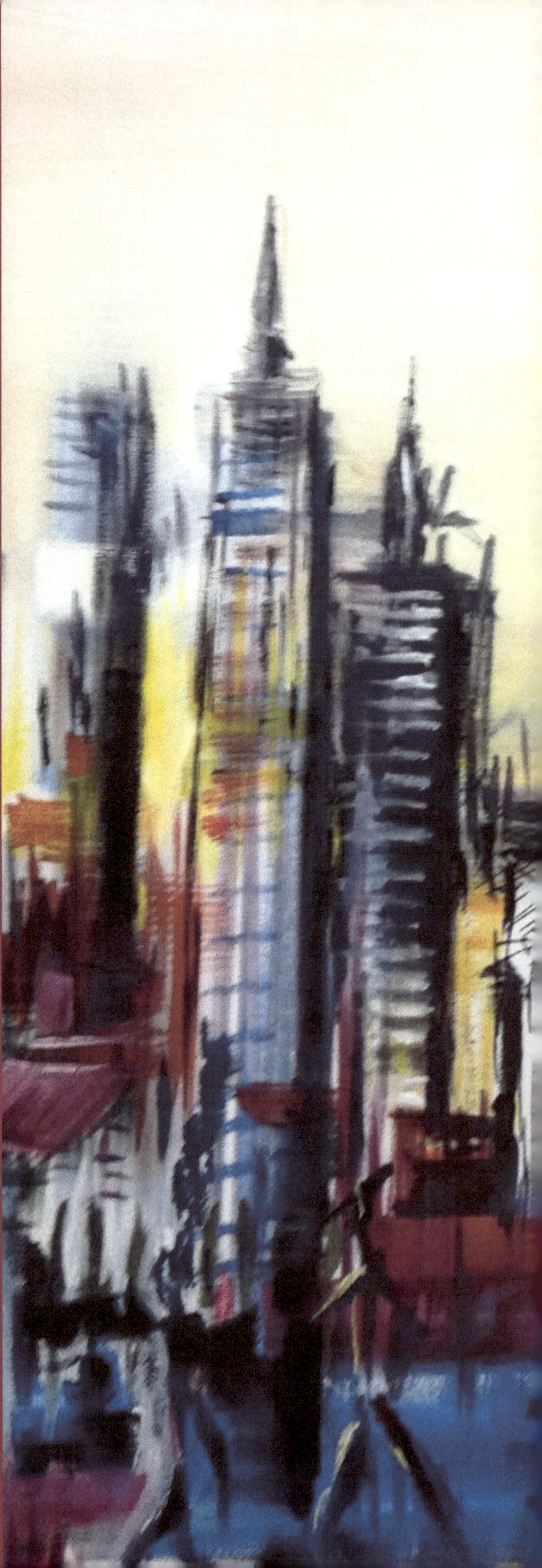

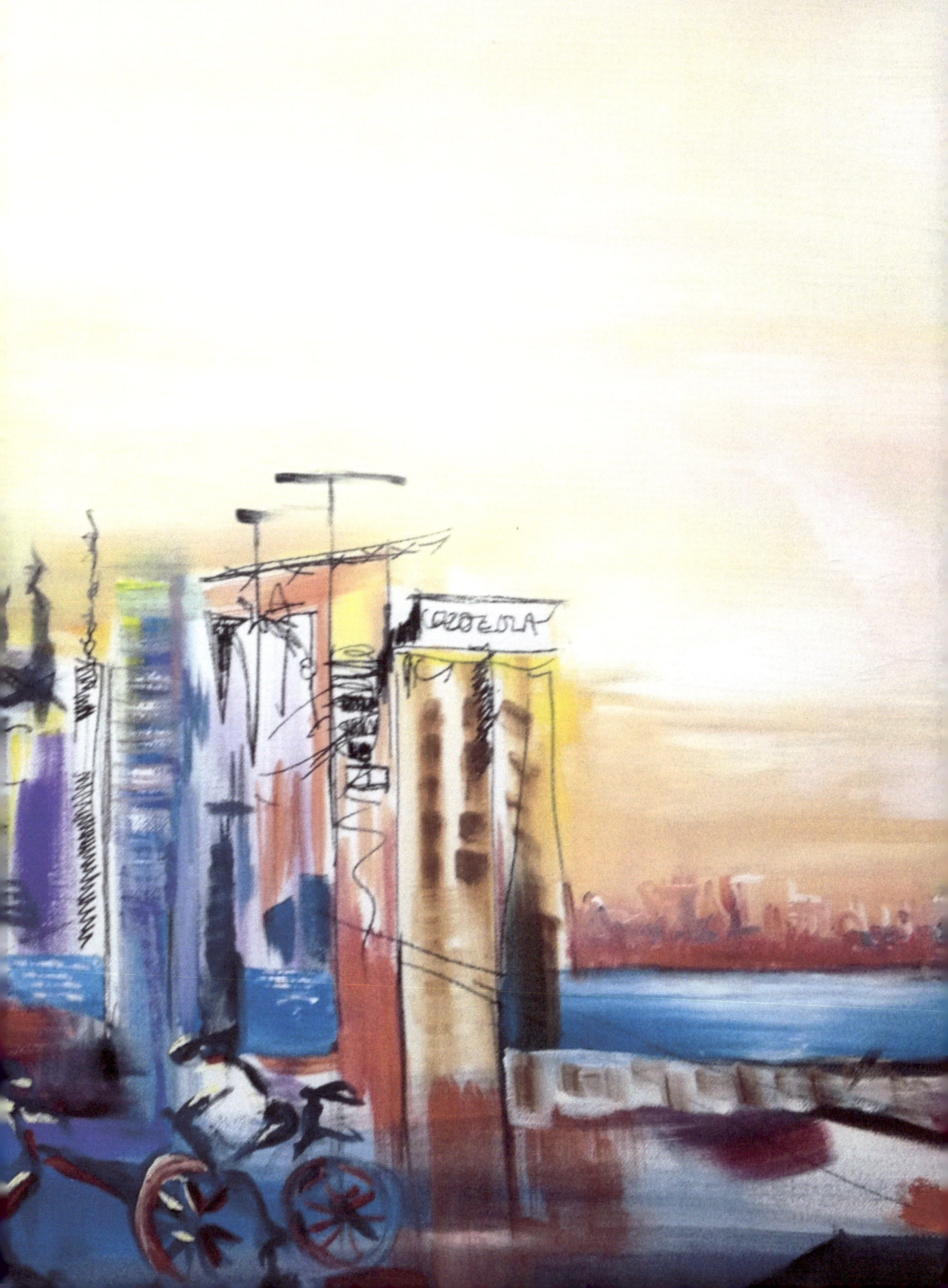

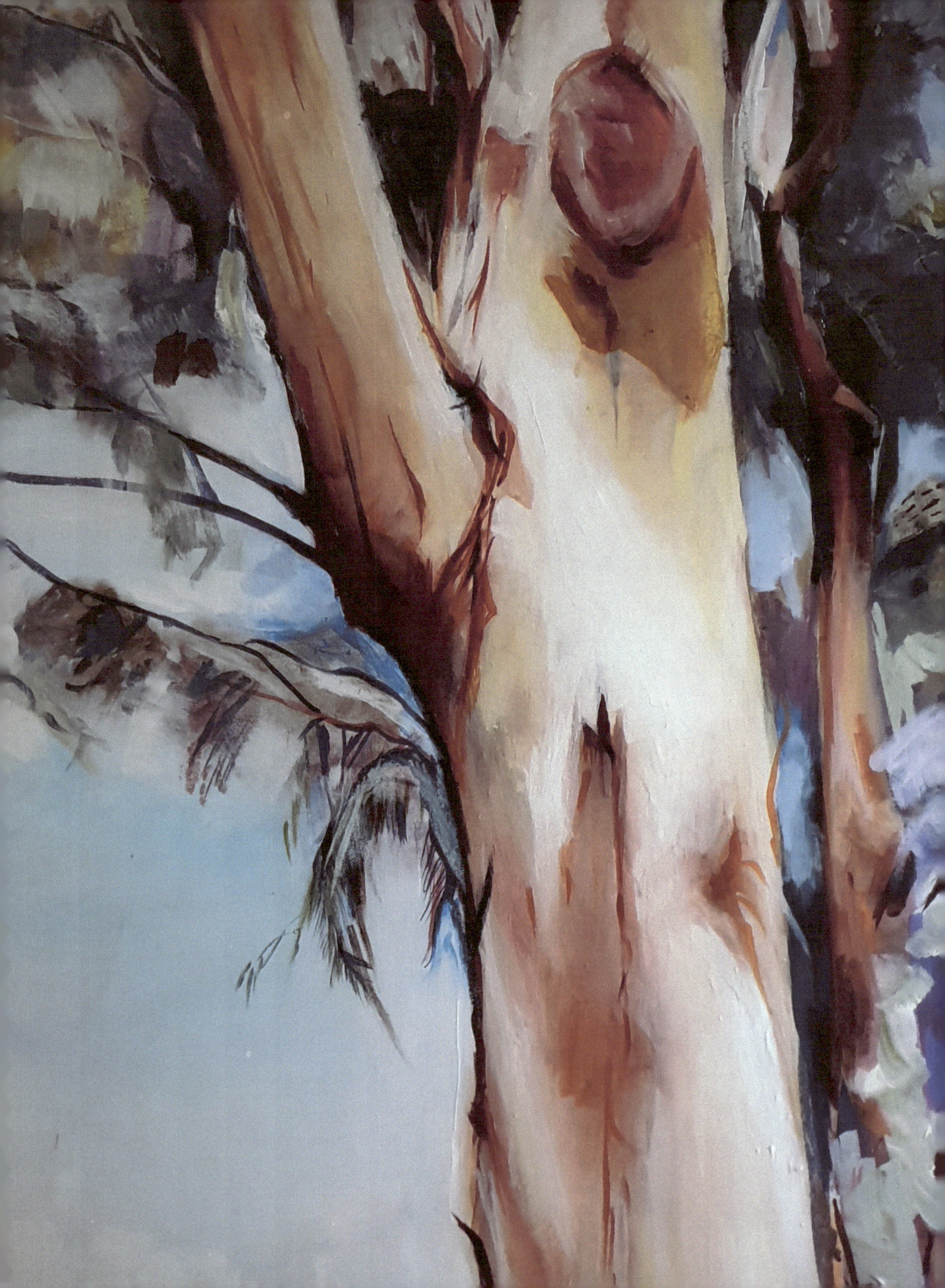

Flourish

My ancestors planted
a pair of blue gums
in the front yard
of our family home
in the hope that
we took roots
like them

Throughout generations
we scattered abroad
to search life's purpose
and explored the world
outside of home's comfort

When life was tough
we drew strength
from the smell of eucalyptus
and sought refuge
in the memory
of our elders foretold
the prosperity to come
with sheer persistence
and a grateful heart

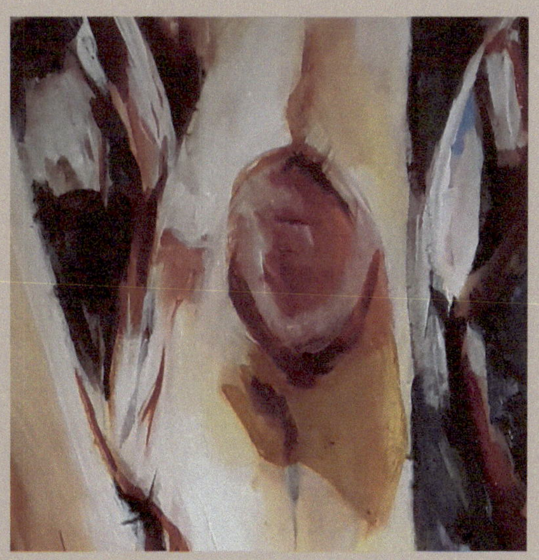

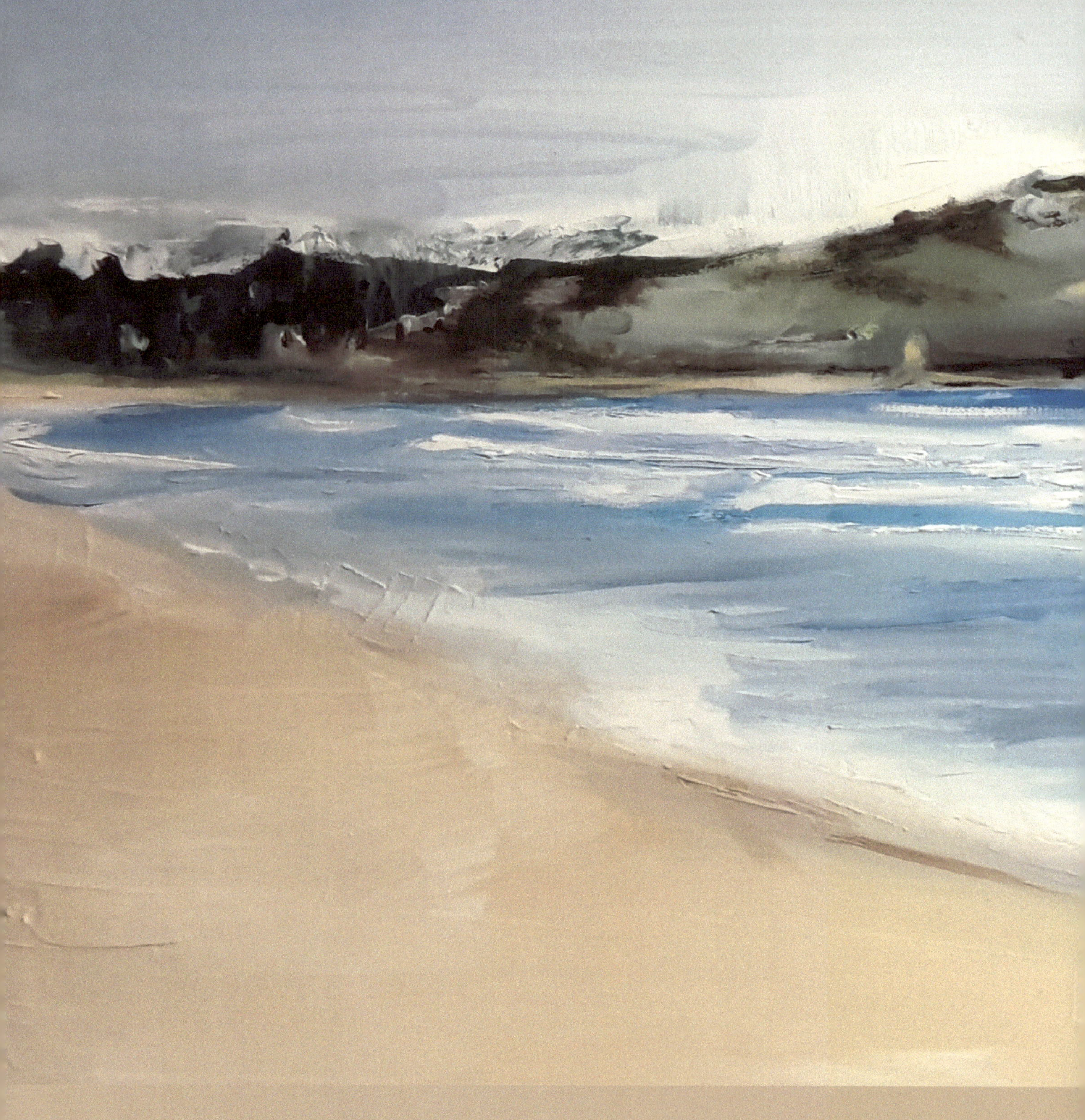

Avalon in siesta

Is where my heart belongs

Farewell sunshine

Before the curtains fall

I am ready to rest

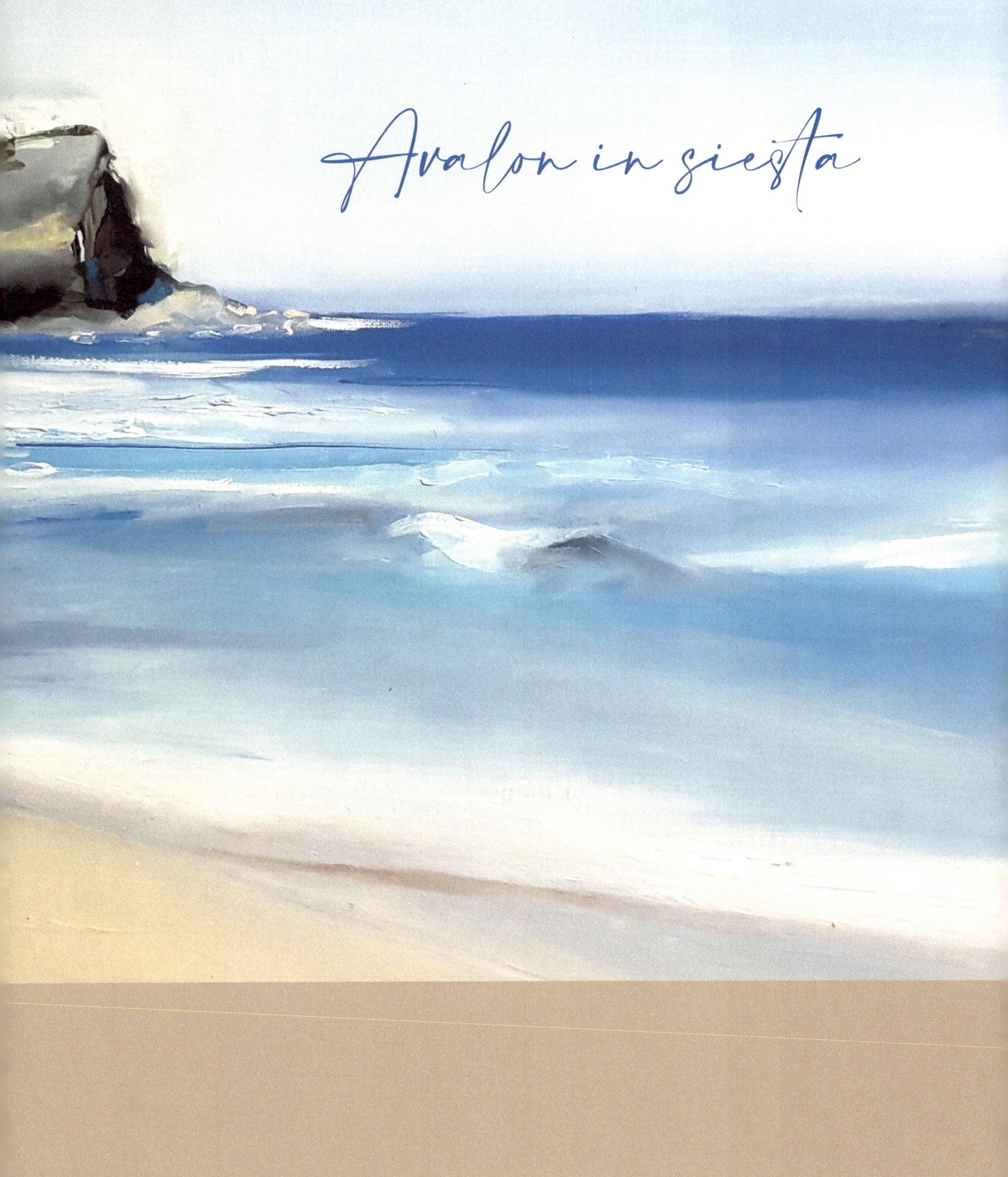
Avalon in siesta

Journey

Together
we grew from riding rocking horses
to raising a family
We loved and nurtured our children
to be their own unique person

Here we are back to where we started
at our old age
being side by side
Nature generously rewards us
for our tireless giving
the sunset sky radiates pink
and yellow on our grey hairlines

You look at me,
I look at you
in sincerity, in serenity
Our journey ends peacefully
at this moment in time

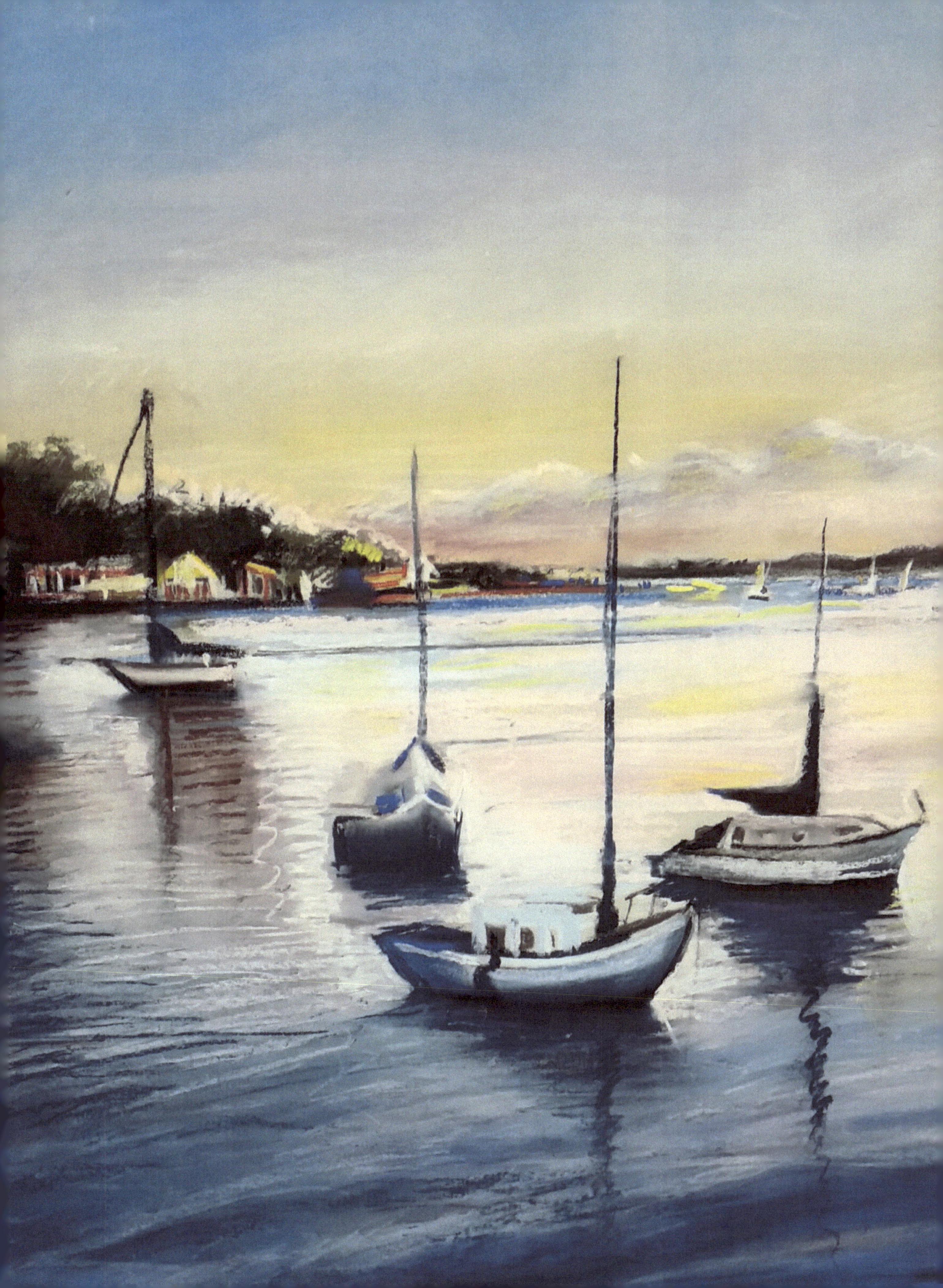

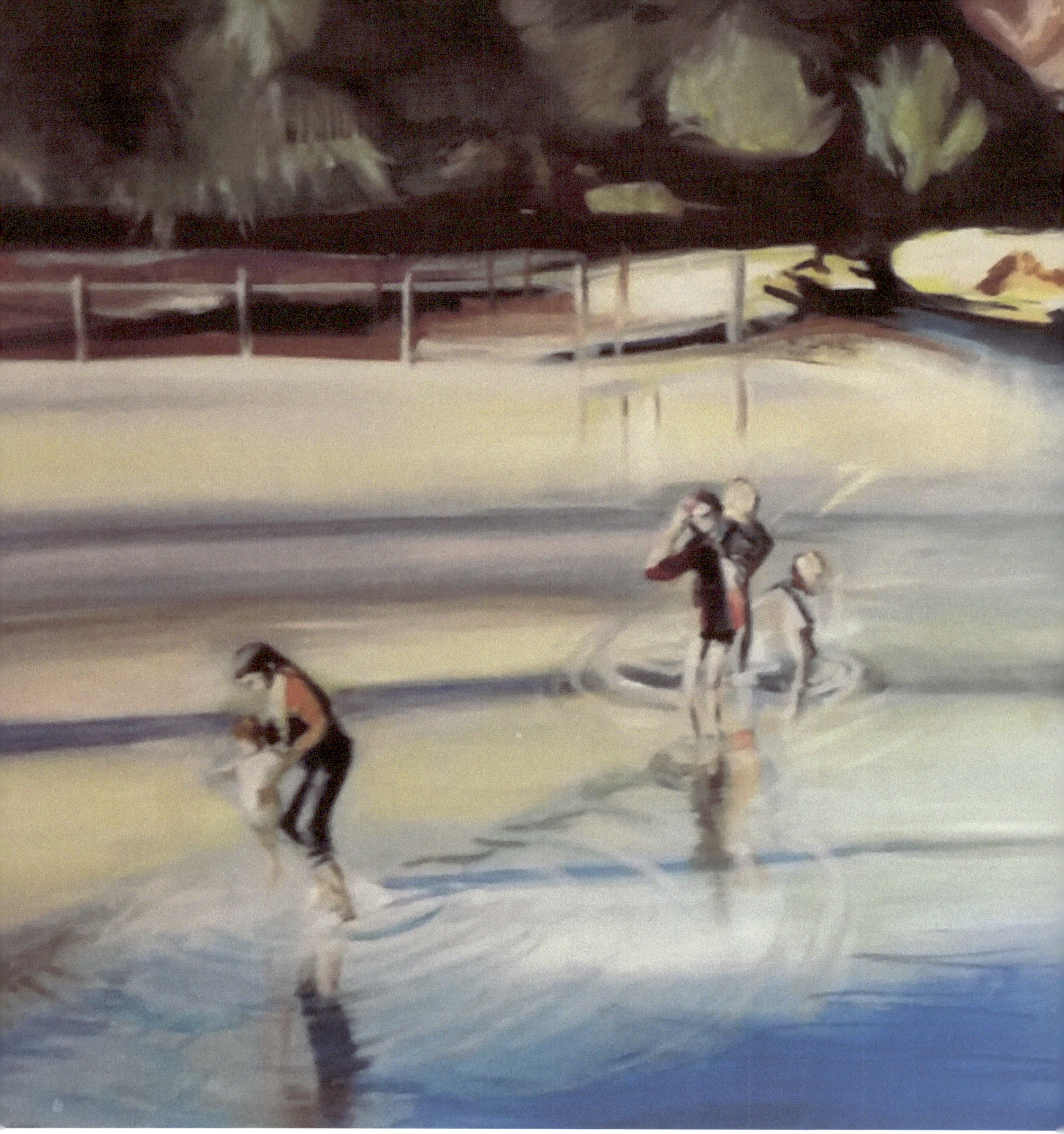

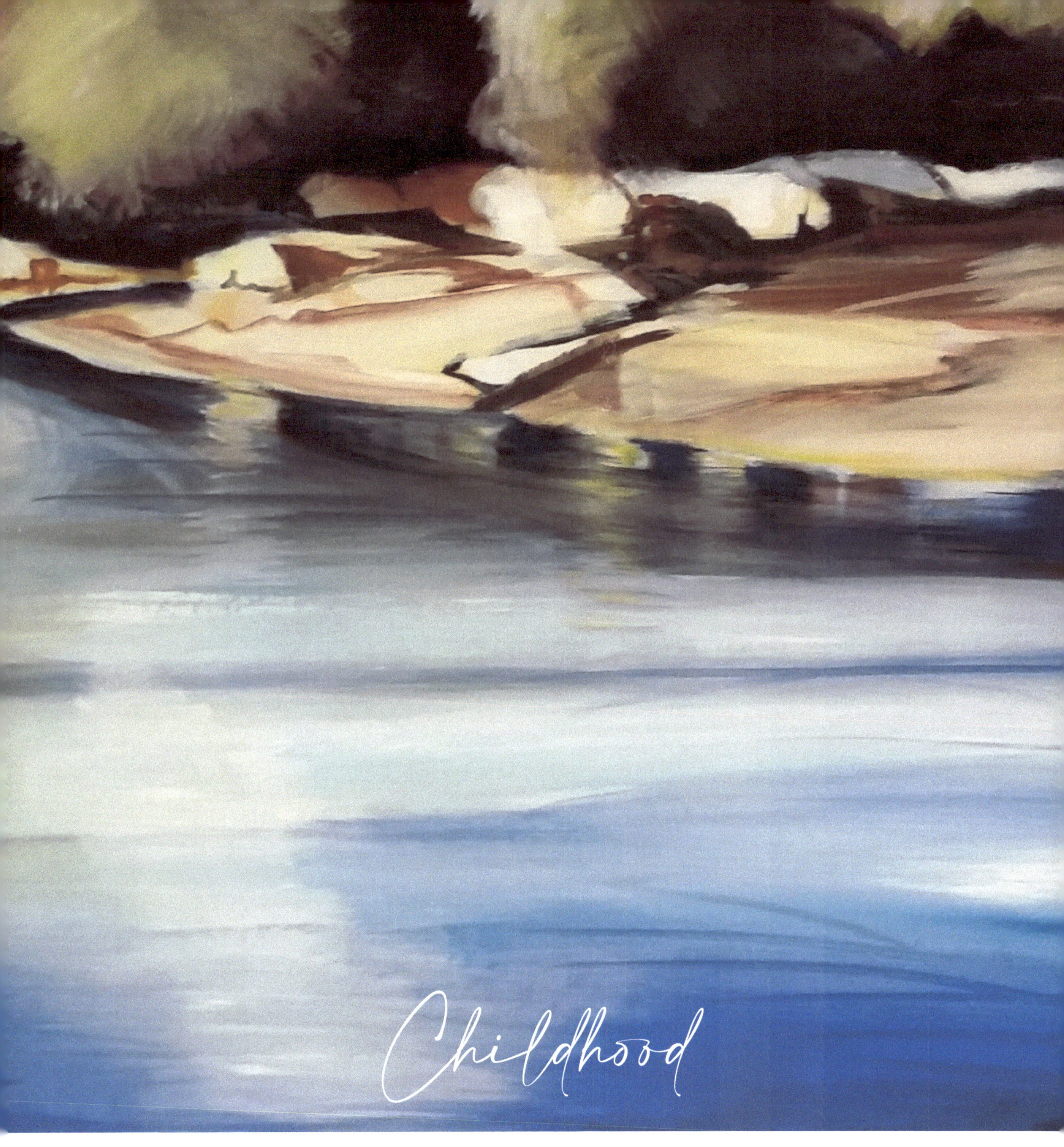

Childhood

I remember those fun beach afternoons
We bathed in the gossamer autumn sun
Daddy's shoulders were the mountains we climbed
Mummy's arms were the swing we clung to
The secluded Clovelly echoed the wonderful childhood
which we locked away in our fond memory

Rush

Looking out the train window

I feel the same rush of time and space

Wheaten open plains move like weeping willows in the wind

Lines of oil rich Eucalyptus trees casting elongated shadows on the land

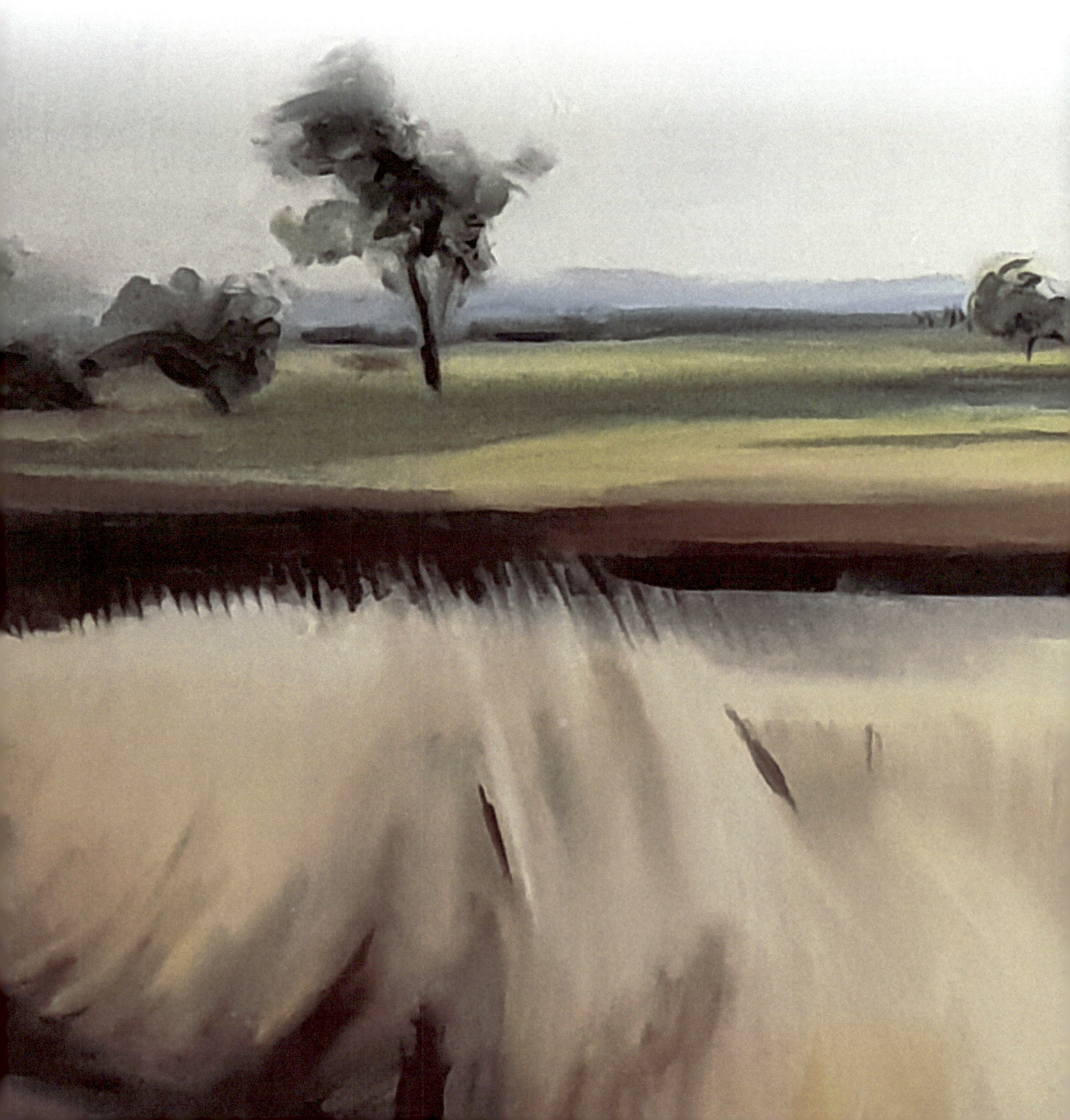

The blue haze mountain backdrop vanishes into the distant clouds

They charge all at once to meet my eyes

Too overwhelmed to take them in frame by frame

I feel the sudden nostalgia of old black and white flicks

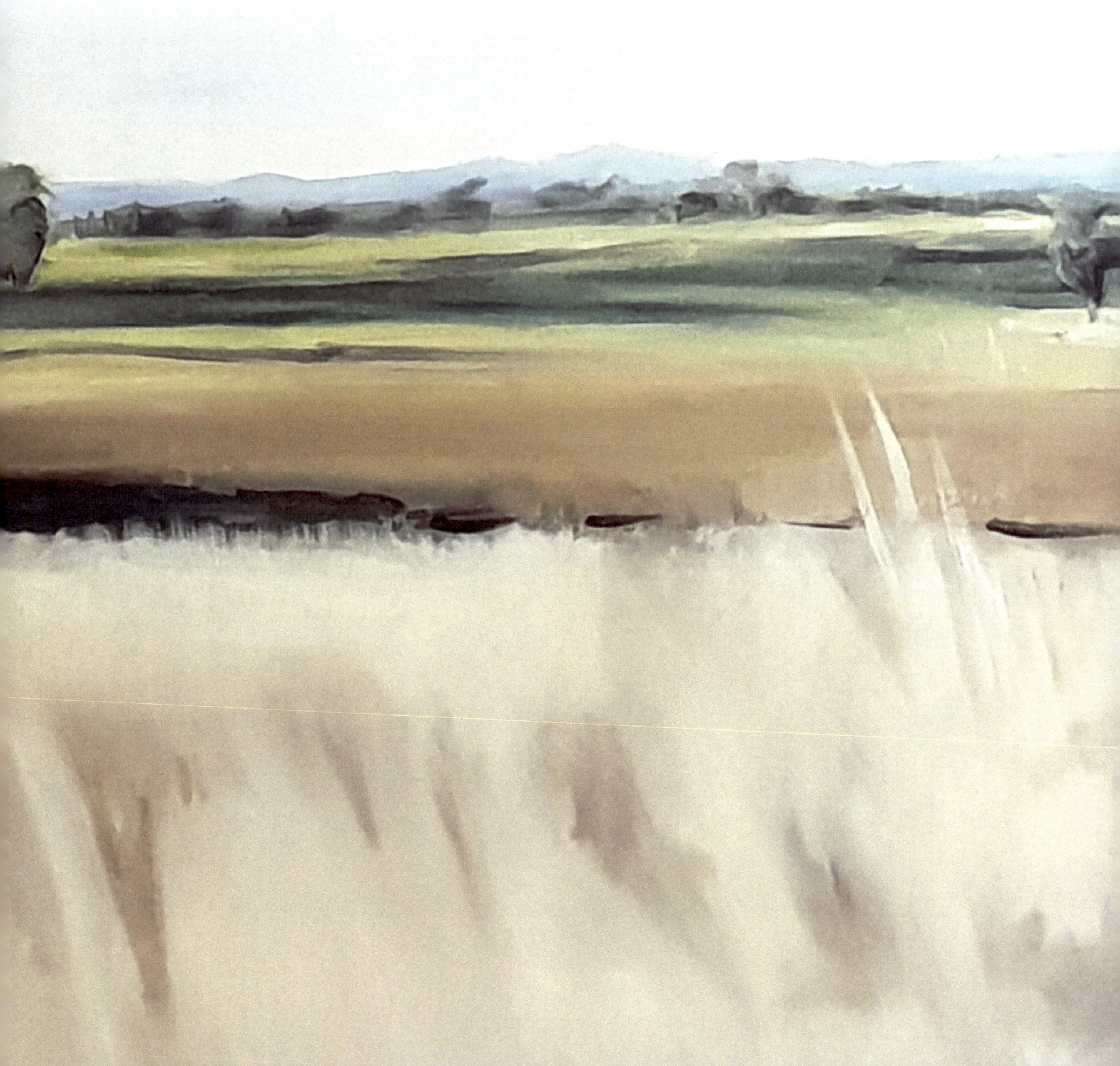

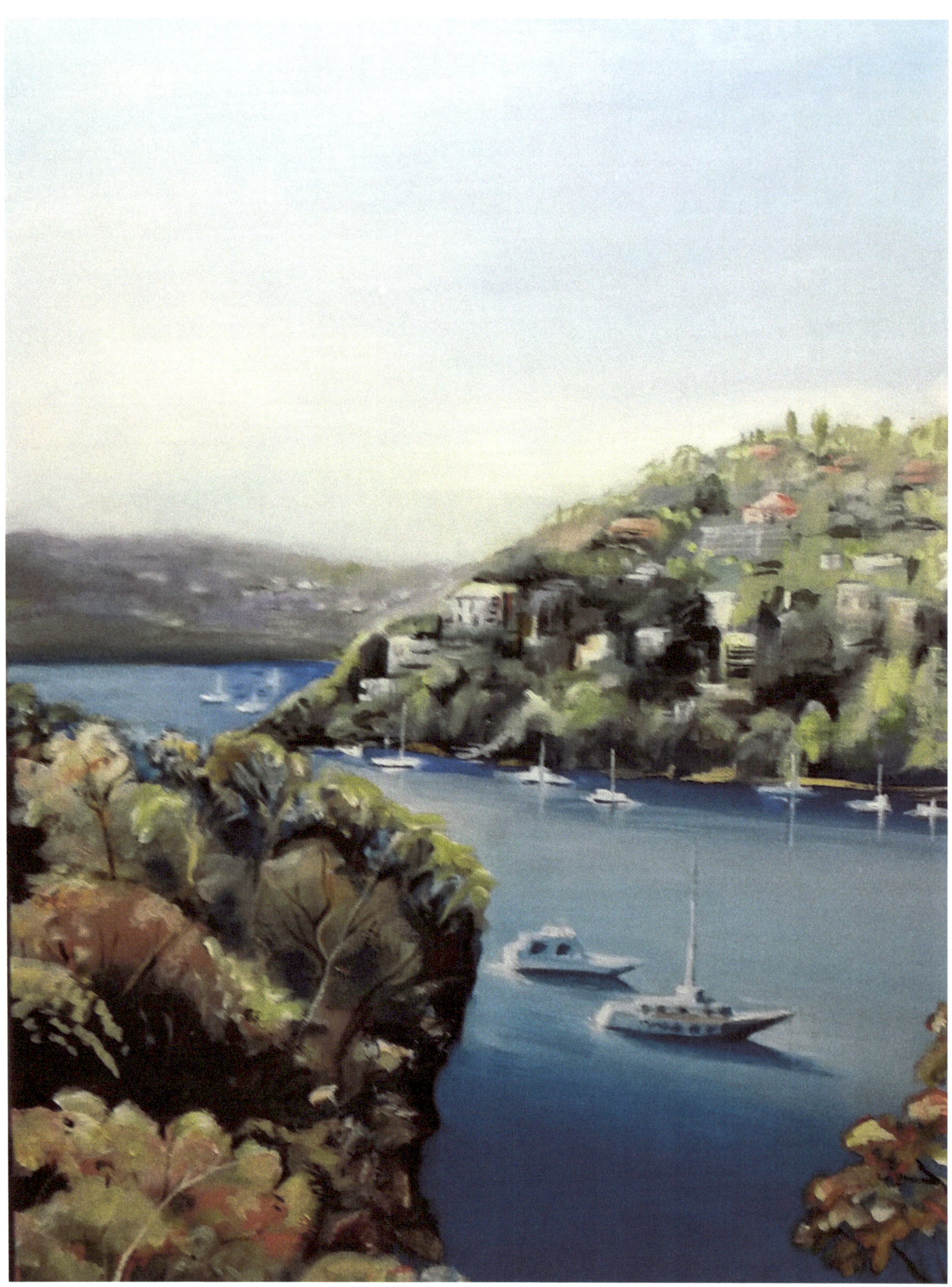

Mosman Bay

The scenery of heath, woodland and forest
showcases the mix palette of native acacia, banksia,
red bloodwood and Sydney peppermint
decorated with newly arrived lantana and privet

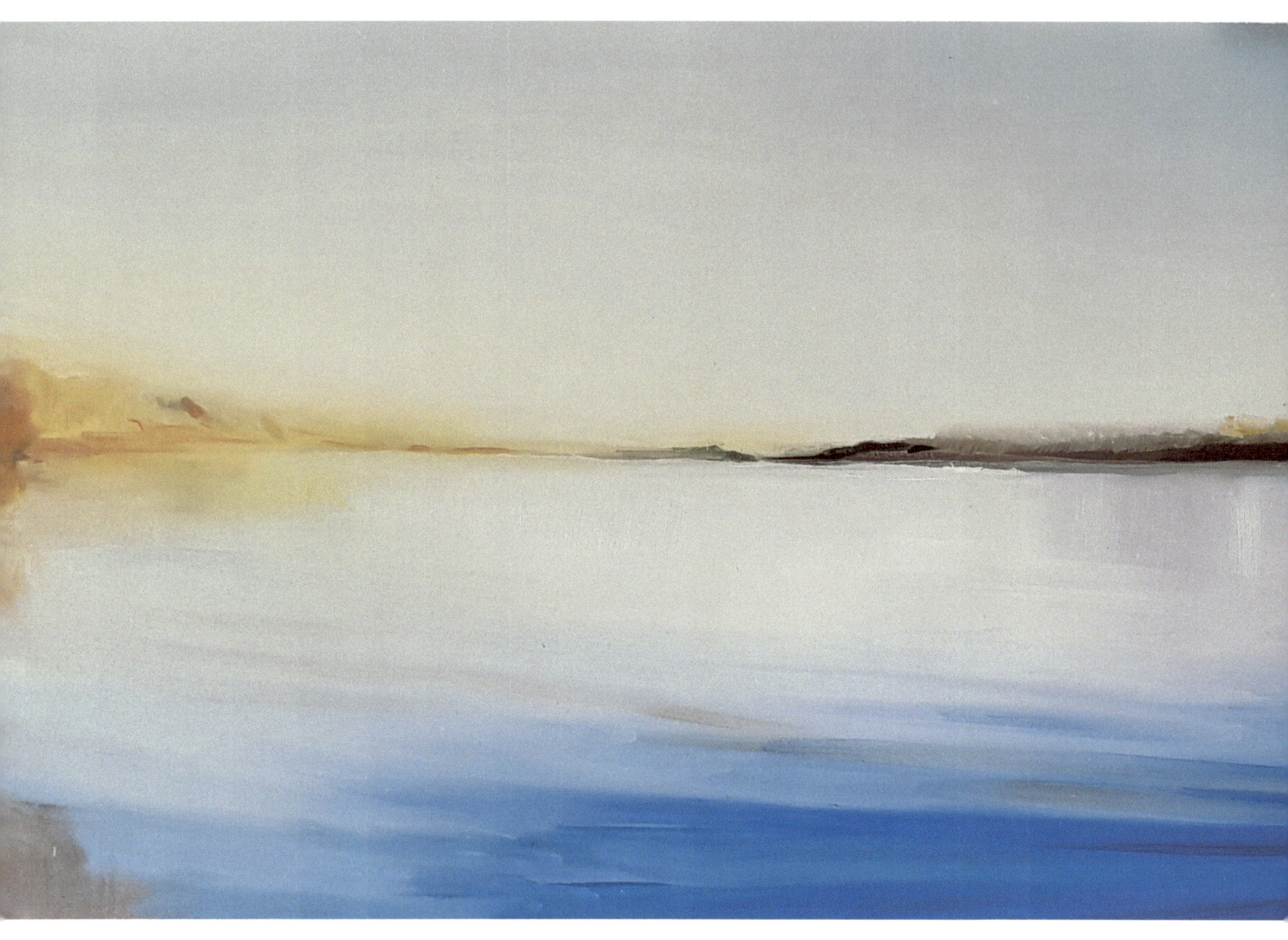

Generations

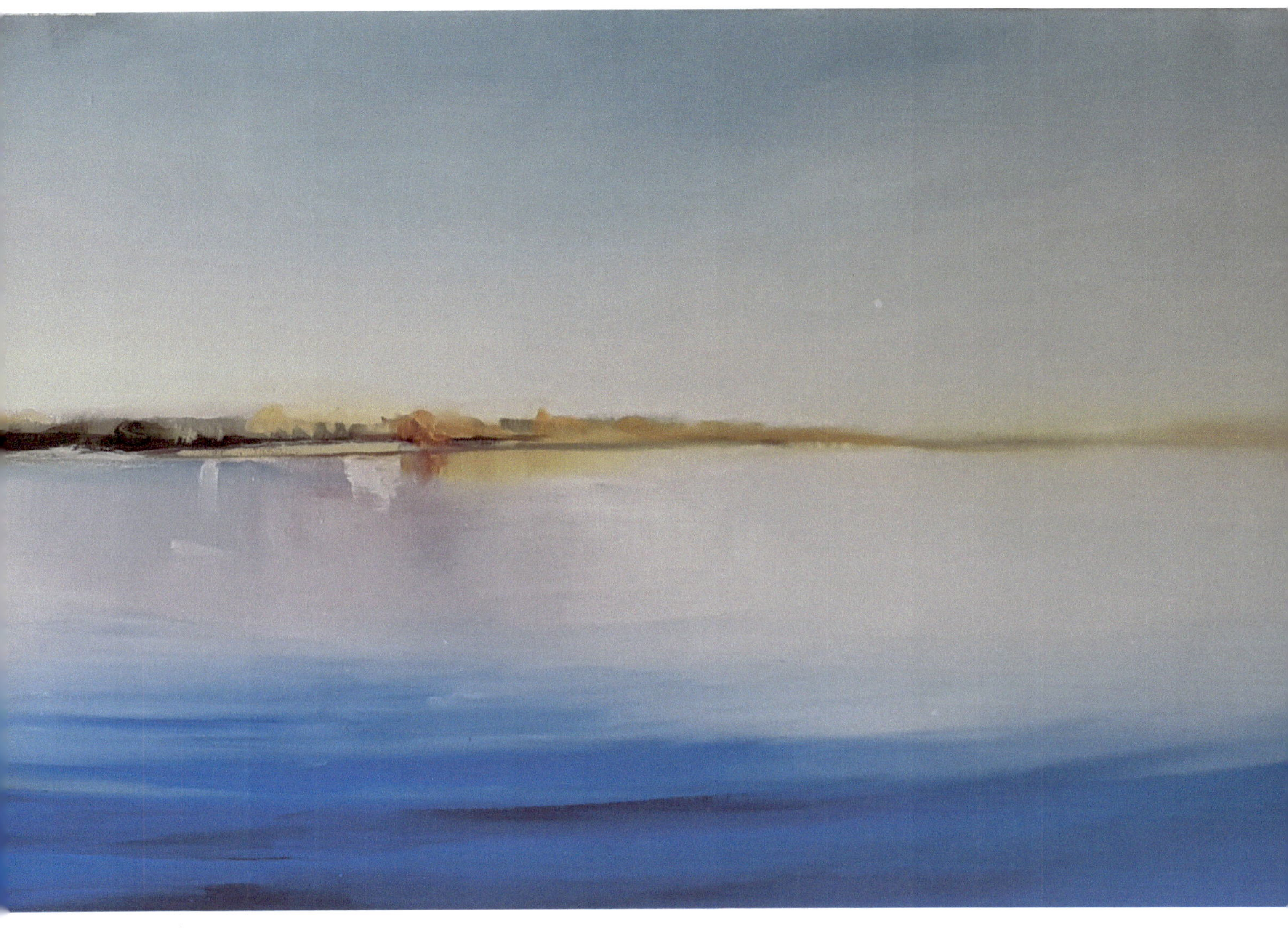

The children left home for the city neon lights
Faces filled with endless enthusiasm
Brushed off sandburs that caught on their jeans
Covered tree scratched wrists with tailored shirts
The bell birds by the river sang their farewell
They never looked back to see your outstretched arms
The silvery grey city edge is where the elders rise early
To wait for the youth to come home

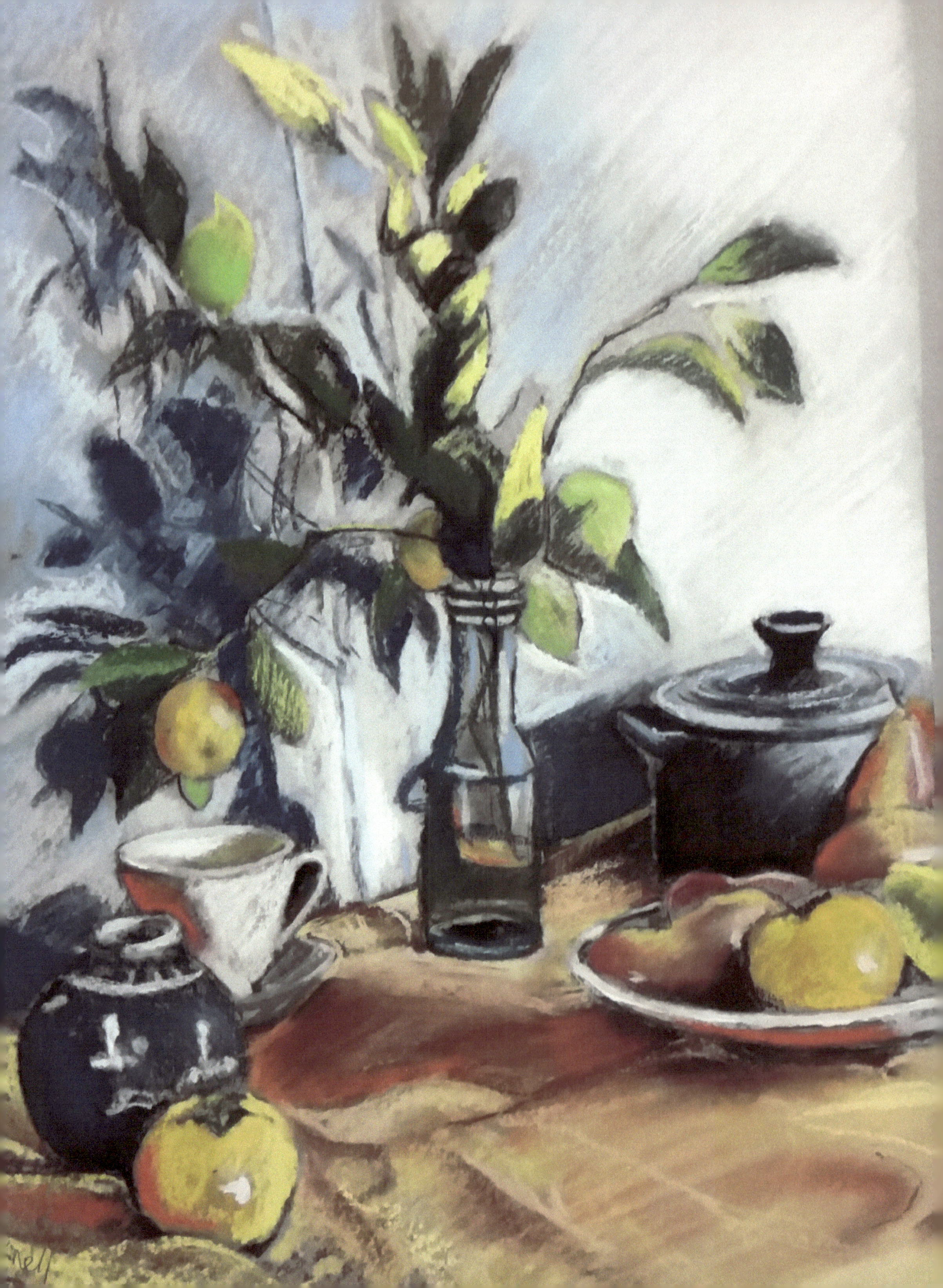

Nana's Kitchen

Walk past the lemon and persimmon trees
Follow the scent trail of French earl grey
My tired eyes sparked
by Nana's broad smile
Throw myself into her wide opened arms
Expect her to rock and tickle me nonstop
I can't help but let out a string of giggles
We kiss each other in affection as always
My grey hairline and crow's feet smiling eyes
meet with Nana's snow-white glory
and crisscrossed gentle gaze
Settle at the rustic farmhouse table
Share a cup of hot tea
in her organic kitchen
just like yesterday
but forever ago

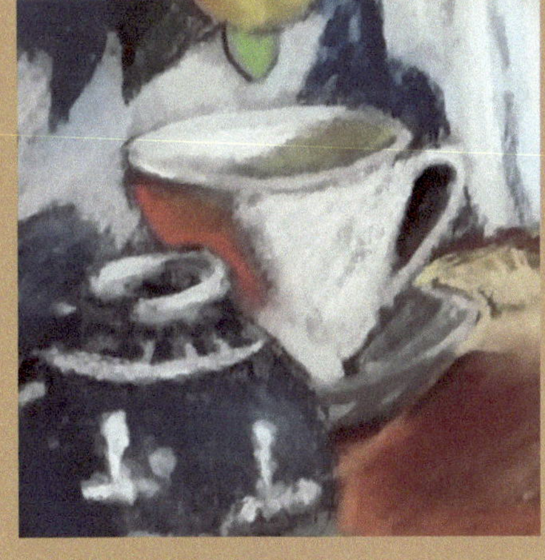

Bedlam Bay

ON A SATURDAY MORNING

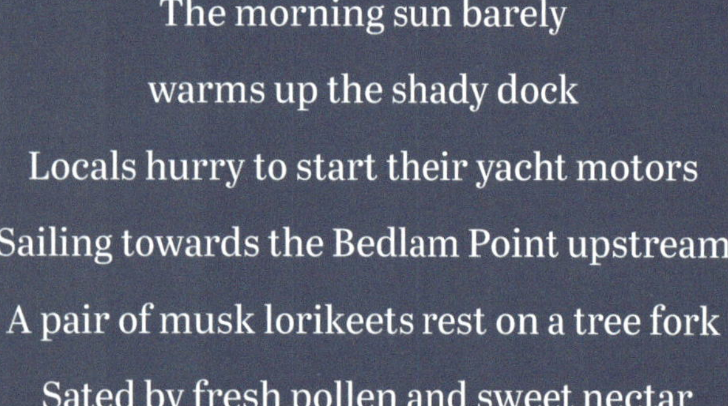

The morning sun barely
warms up the shady dock
Locals hurry to start their yacht motors
Sailing towards the Bedlam Point upstream
A pair of musk lorikeets rest on a tree fork
Sated by fresh pollen and sweet nectar
The river bathes in an azure daydream

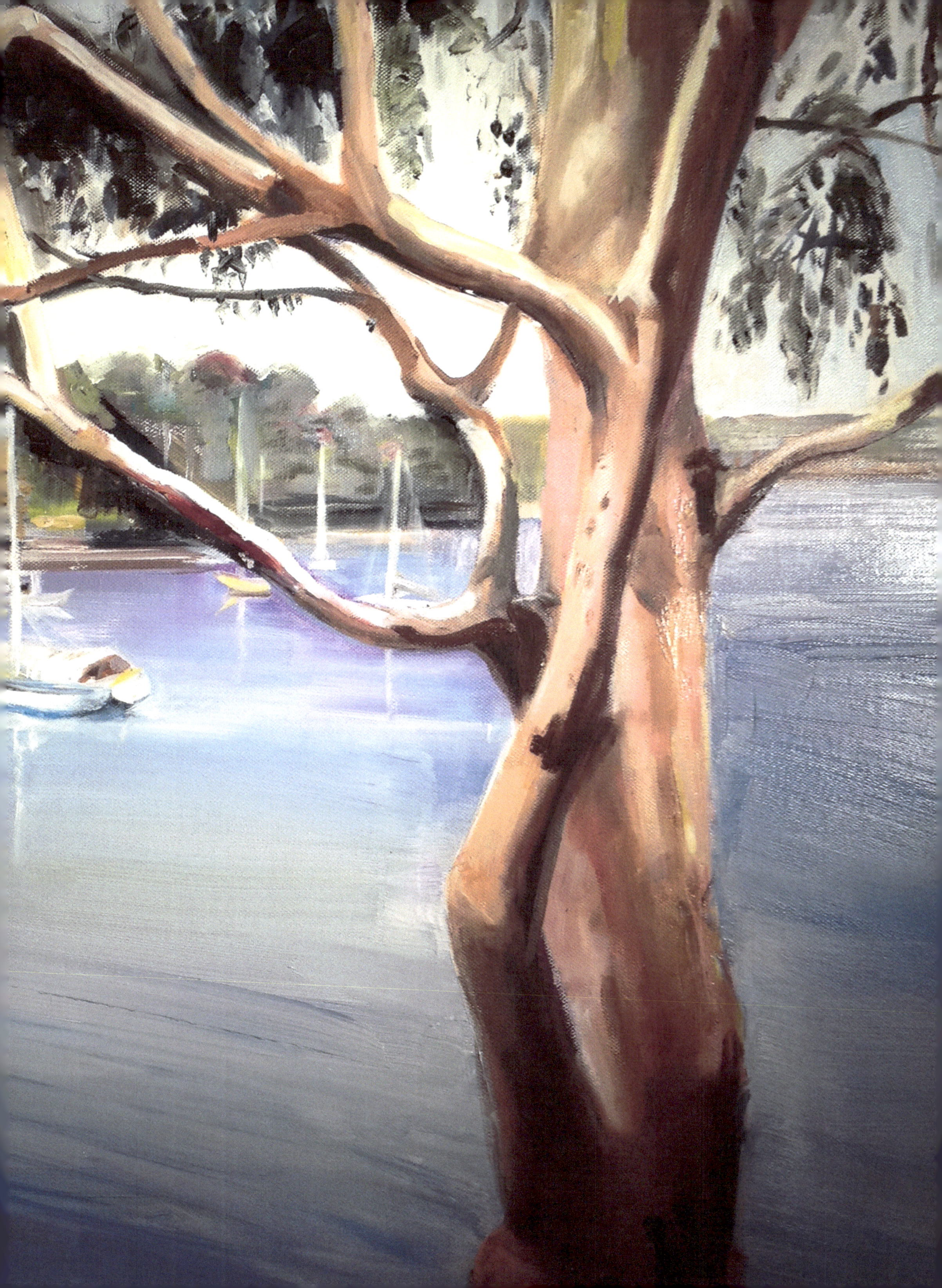

Falling in Love

I bundled every blooming flower
from my overgrown garden
to try to impress you
You accepted them with delight,
arranged them in a vase
and preserved their vibrancy
with a palette of colours
and linseed oil
I witnessed a gifted artist
fervently creating a masterpiece
I knew
I was in love with you

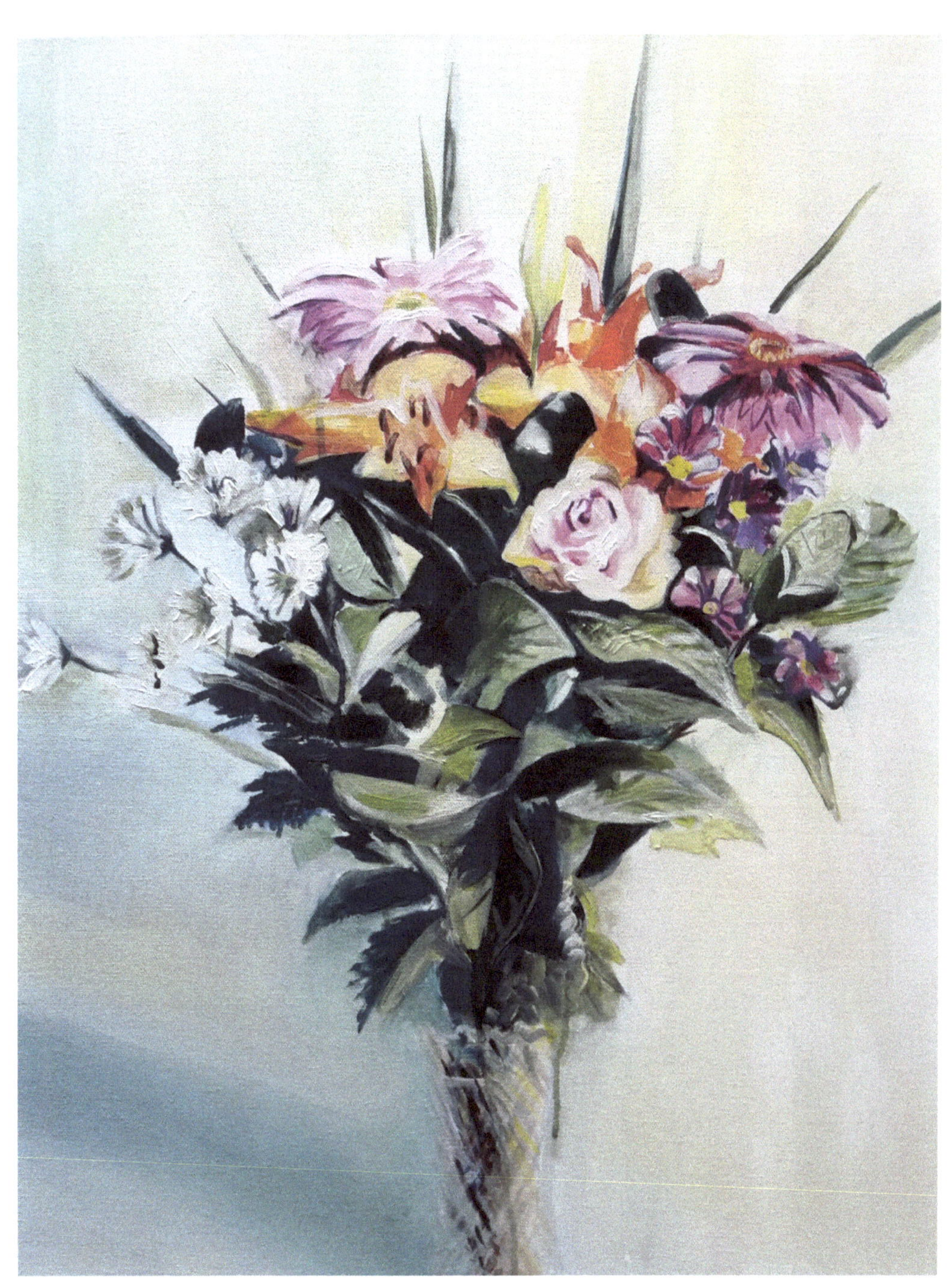

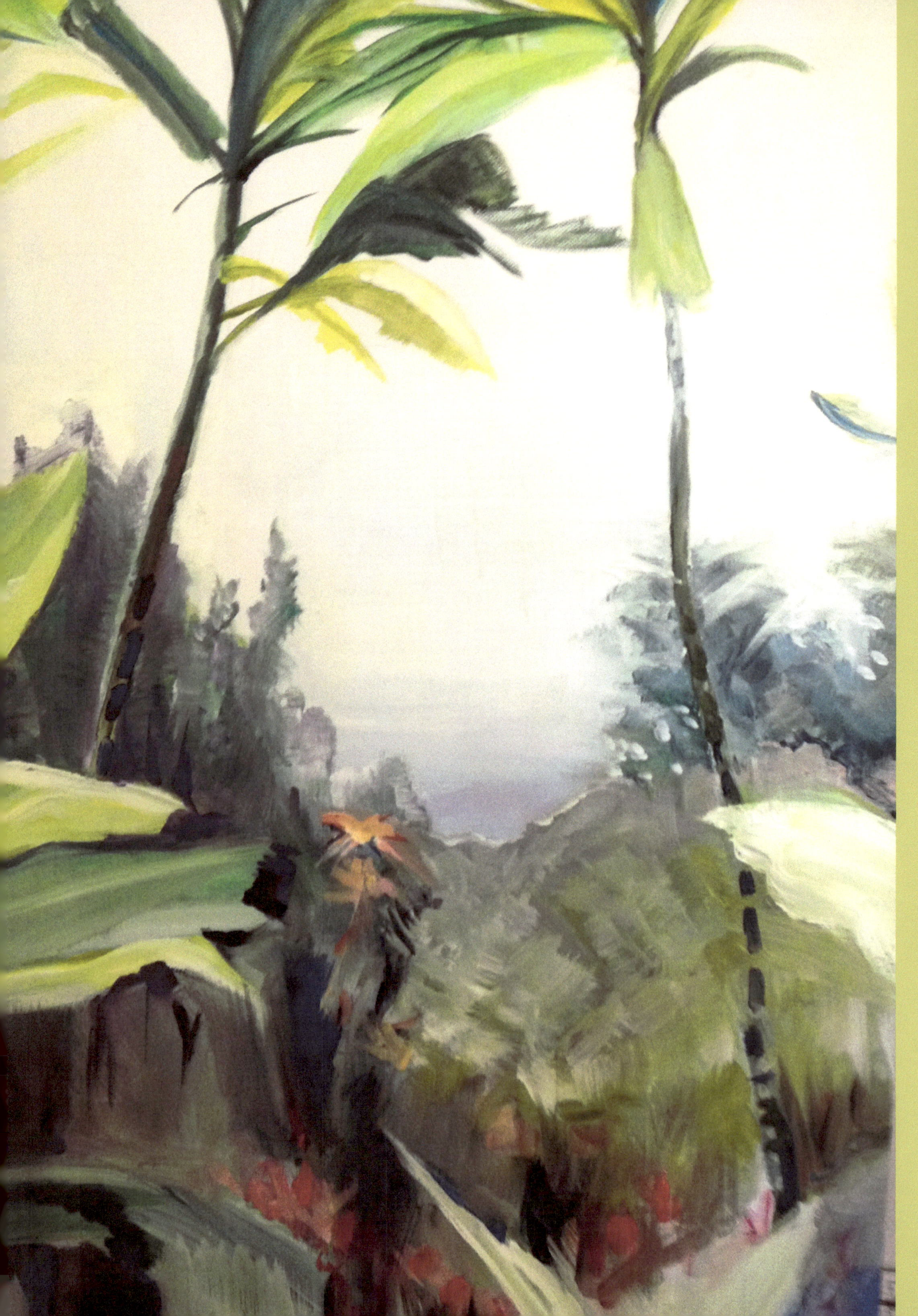

Choice

Tread upon unknown ground
where thorn never grows
and the thistle never springs up

My instinct tells me
to follow the guiding light
Narrow is the way to paradise

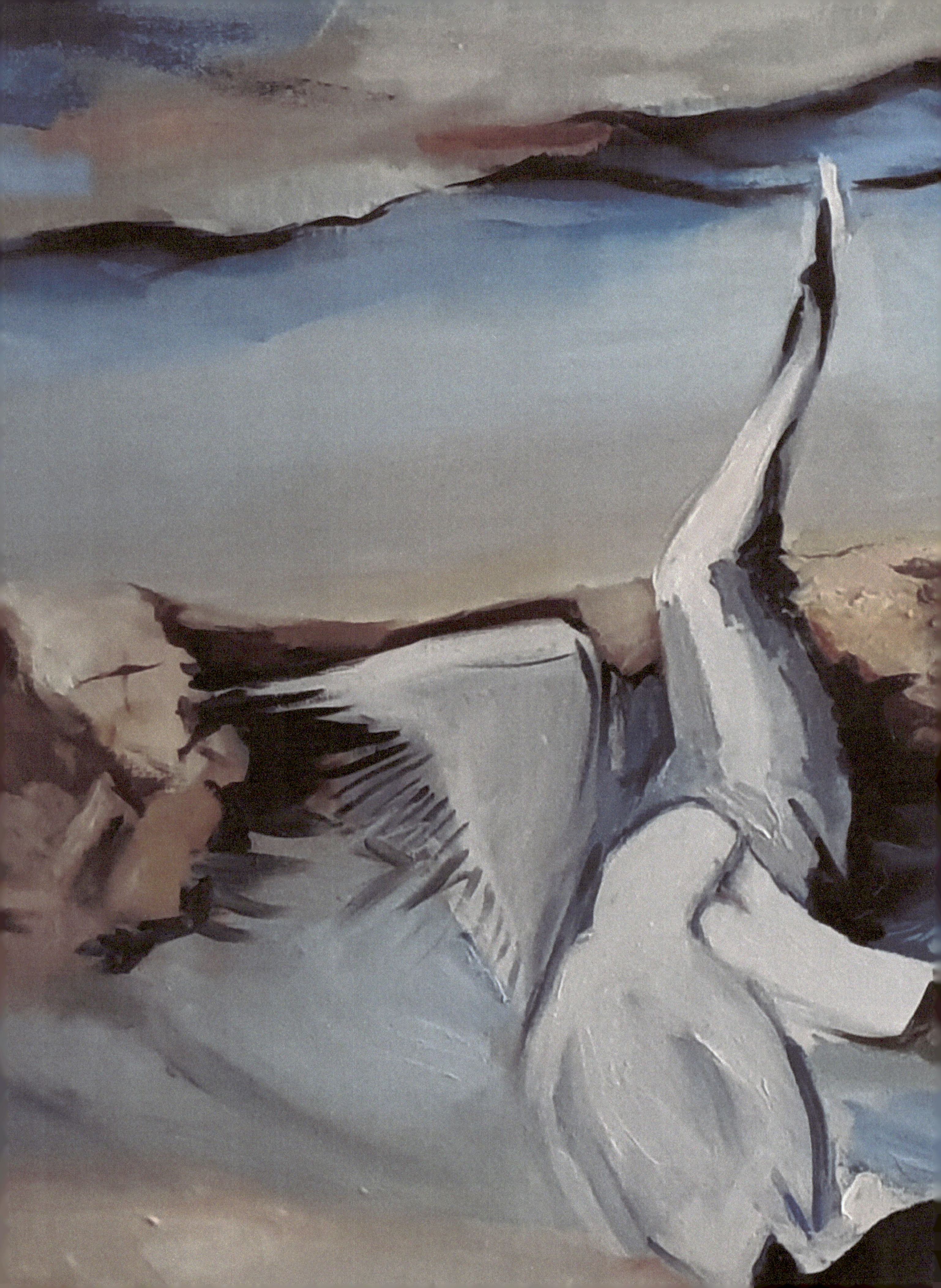

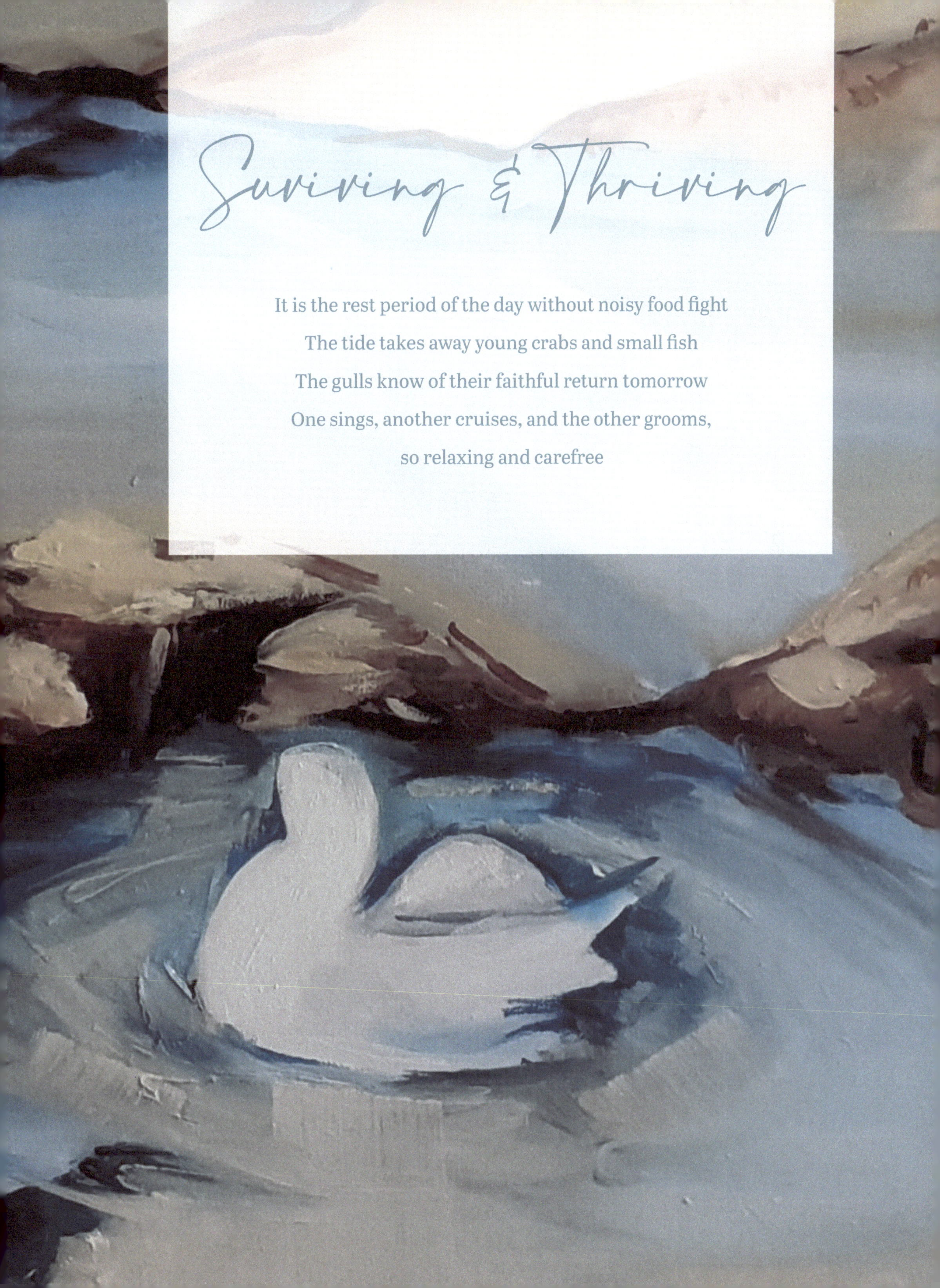

Surviving & Thriving

It is the rest period of the day without noisy food fight
The tide takes away young crabs and small fish
The gulls know of their faithful return tomorrow
One sings, another cruises, and the other grooms,
so relaxing and carefree

Secluded Clovelly Beach

Their warmth pushes the native shrubs to absorb
the aqua calm waves into teal

The nature's palette sets an energetic backdrop
for a family fun time

The sand shimmers like lemon zest
surprising the children with playful splashing

Laughter echoes off the rocks like a baby
mumbles into their mother's arm,
cheerful in Clovelly's embrace

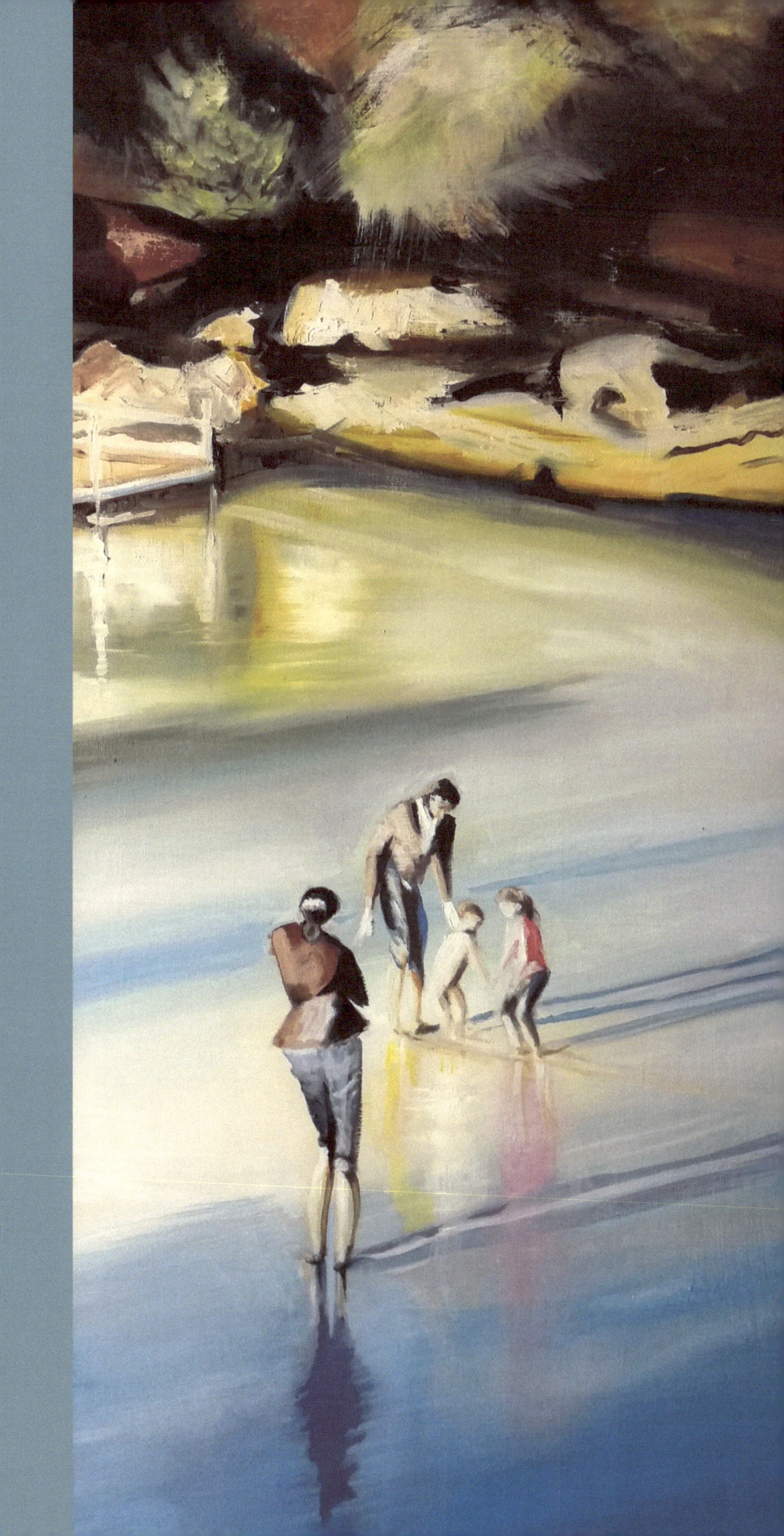

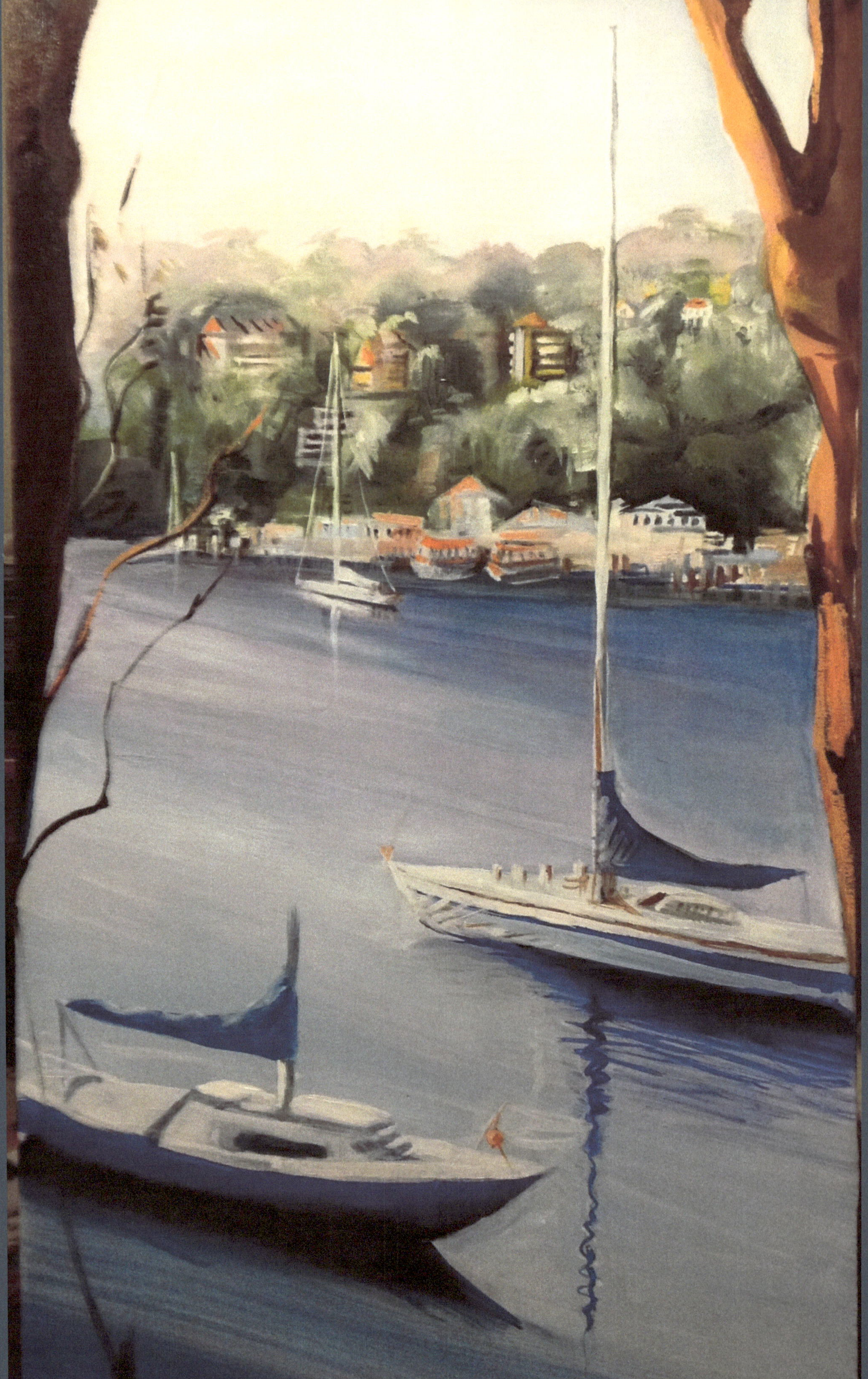

Sanctuary

This used to be our secret place
Where the still water was stirred
by our rosy kisses
Frantic hands hidden
in the bush laden inlet

Sacred kingfishers were jealous
of our playfulness
Darting through the green
and grey branches

Pied cormorants were watchful
of the riverbank
The green and blue river rippled
perfect reflection of their orbs
We sailed our yacht along
the stretched yellow mangrove
Left our sanctuary behind
in the tangerine sunset

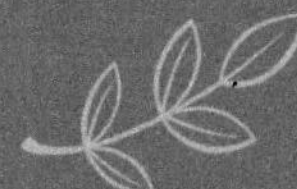

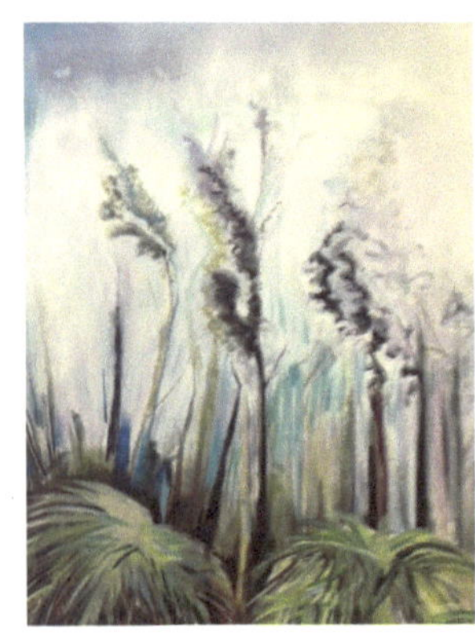
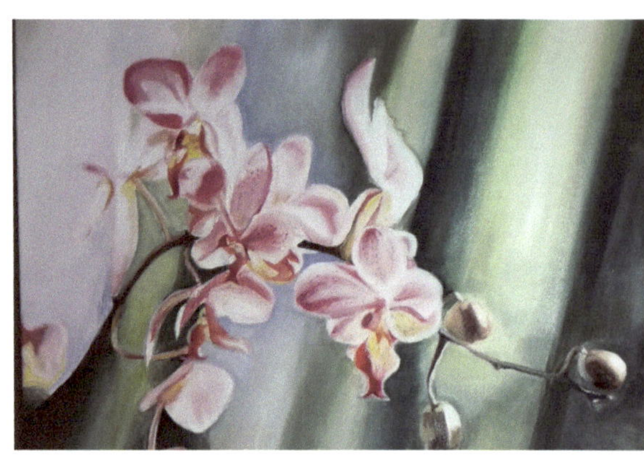
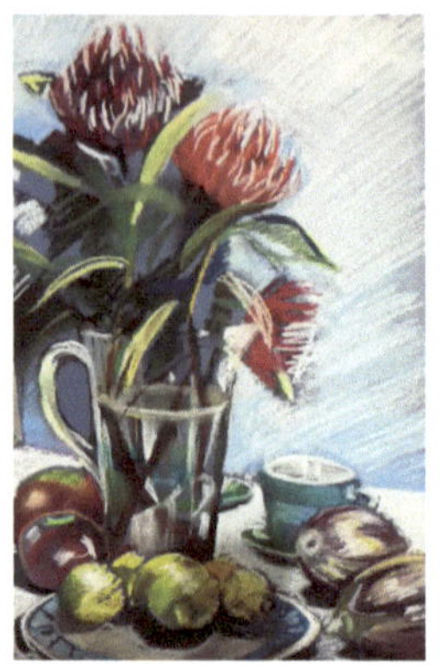
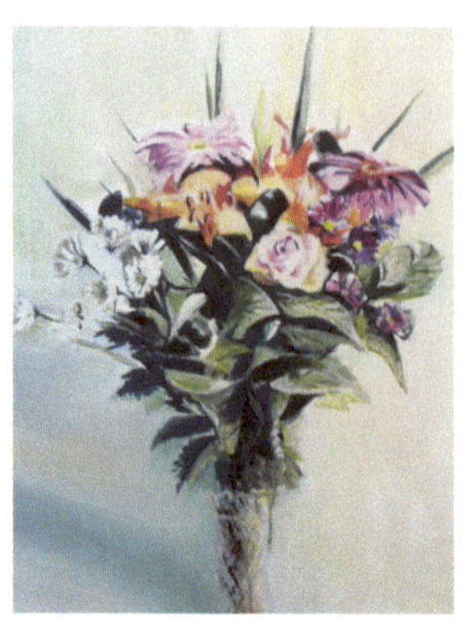
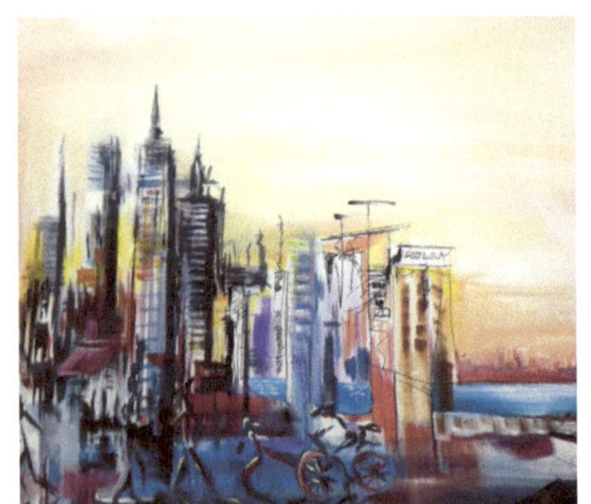
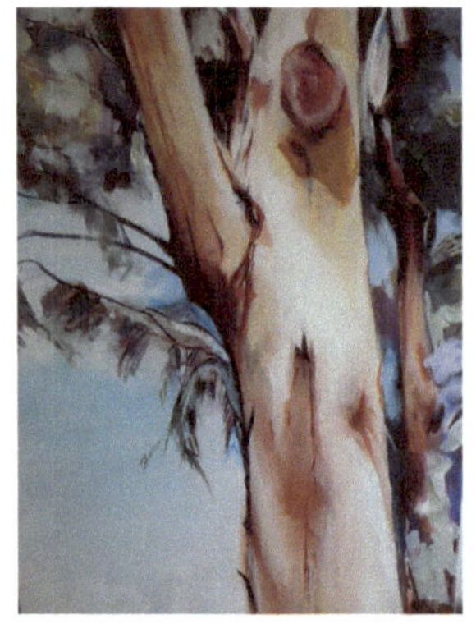
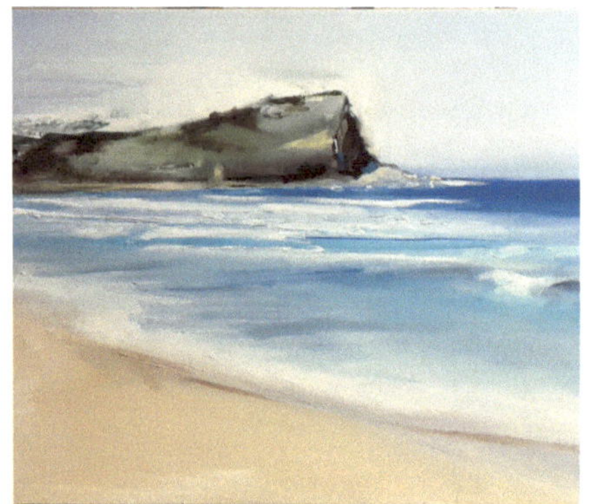
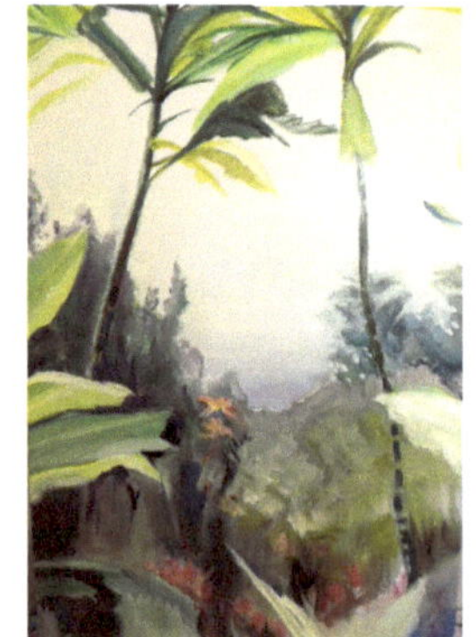
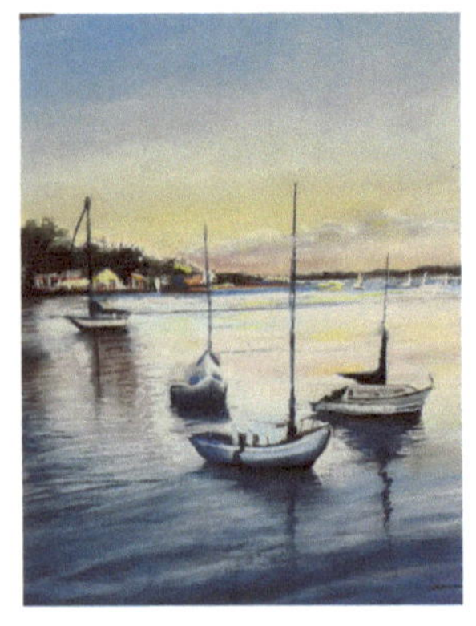
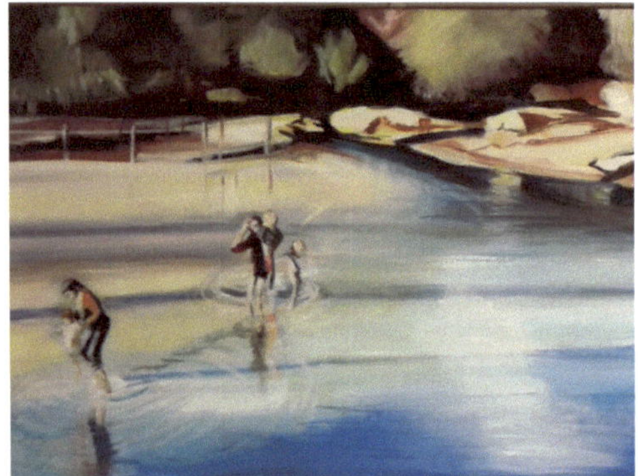
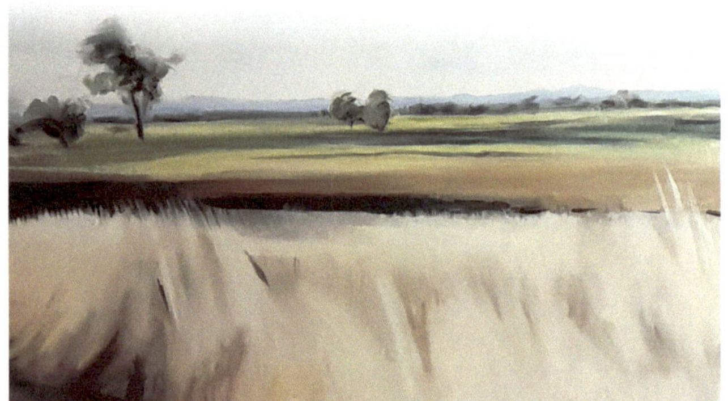
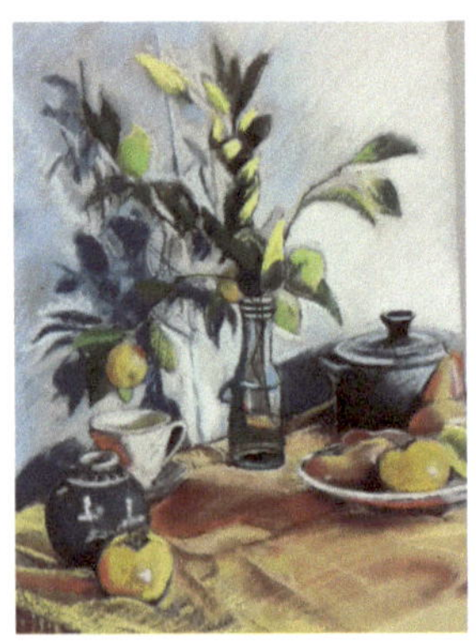
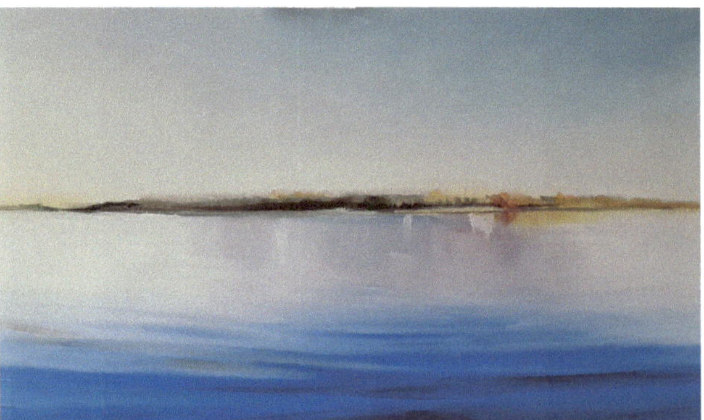
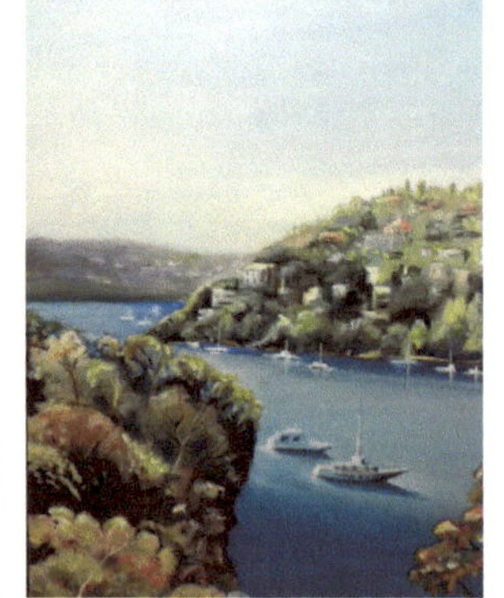
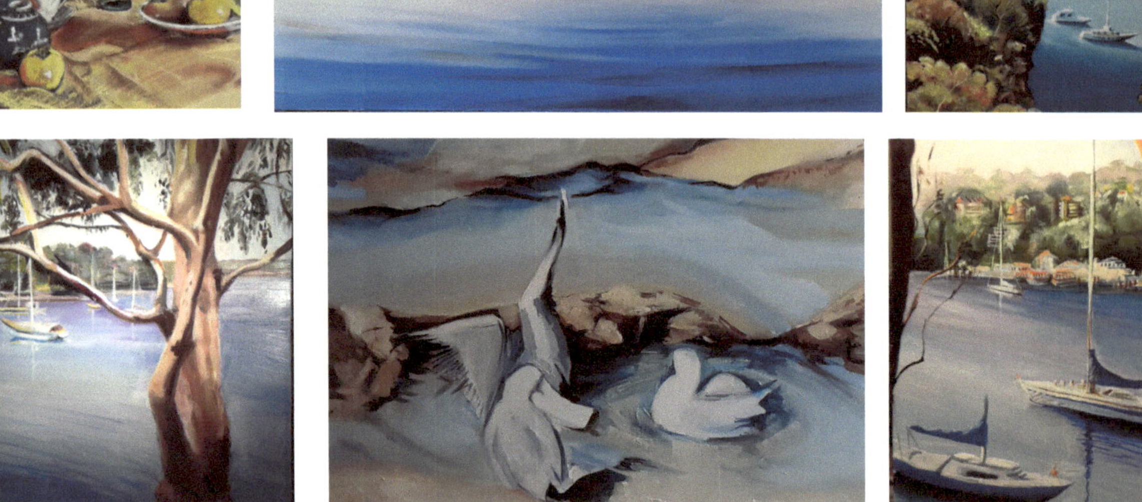
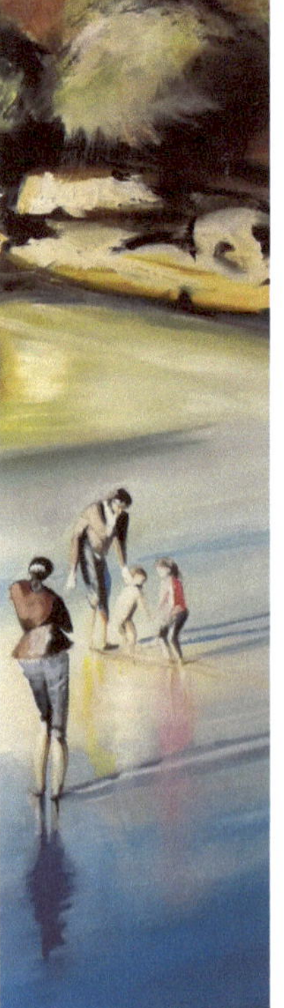